John Beattie Crozier

Lord Randolph Churchill, a study of England democracy

John Beattie Crozier

Lord Randolph Churchill, a study of England democracy

ISBN/EAN: 9783337261399

Printed in Europe, USA, Canada, Australia, Japan

Cover: Foto ©Suzi / pixelio.de

More available books at **www.hansebooks.com**

LORD RANDOLPH CHURCHILL.

By the same Author.

CIVILIZATION AND PROGRESS,

Being the outlines of a New System of Political, Religious, and Social Philosophy.

14s.

PRESS NOTICES.

"An original thinker and a clear, forcible writer."—*Scotsman.*

"This is a work of real ability. It is full of thought, and its style is both forcible and clear. The reader is borne on a stream of strong thinking from point to point, until at last, when he pauses to get a little mental breath, he finds that he has been doing almost as much thinking as the author himself, so stimulating and suggestive is the book; and so full is it of discriminating, vigorous, and subtle ideas."—*Inquirer.*

"There can be no doubt, we think, that Mr. Crozier has put his finger upon the weak point in the speculations of previous writers, and that he has himself laid hold of the right method for the adequate treatment of his subject. . . . The work is one of real and pre-eminent merit, and will deservedly take a high place in the class of literature to which it belongs."—*Scottish Review.*

"The ability of Mr. Crozier consists in a remarkable clearness of detail vision, ... fine critical observation, ... singular acumen of distinction—the power, so to speak, of seeing through millstones, of being in a manner clairvoyant. . . . . This accurate and subtle thinker."—Vernon Lee in the *Academy.*

"The book of a very able man. . . . . The testimony which we are compelled to give to the high ability of this ambitious work is completely impartial. . . We can have no doubt as to the great ability of the book, nor as to the literary power with which the thoughts it contains are often expressed. . . . . Full of original criticism. . . . . Great literary faculty. . . . . It will rectify much that is faulty in the views of his predecessors. . . . . A book far less superficial than Mr. Buckle's."—*Spectator.*

By the same Author.

THE RELIGION OF THE FUTURE.

Crown 8vo. 6s.

PRESS NOTICES.

"One of the most powerful of Emerson's sympathetic exponents is Crozier, in his 'Religion of the Future.'"—COOKE'S *Life of Emerson.*

"Mr. Crozier has at least the credit of striking out a path as yet nearly untrodden. He walks in it with steady step, and shows himself a competent guide to others."—*Liverpool Herald.*

"His thoughts are massive and granite-like in their strength. His principles draw deep and reach far. His system as a whole is one which, when duly wrought out and weighed, cannot but carry conviction on the main point for which he contends. . . . A luminous, sure path by which to pass from the region of the Material to the Spiritual, or in other words from Force to God."—*Glasgow Christian Herald.*

"He has helped to unite religious thinkers of all classes in a common stand against Materialism and Atheism."—*Literary World.*

"An able dissertation against Atheism."—*Secular Review.*

"Mr. Crozier considers that the leading causes in philosophy and life which have prevented a harmonious view of the World, may be arranged under four heads. 1. The neglect of the *scale* in the mind. 2. The attempt to account for the World from *without* instead of from *within*. 3. The confusion in the choice of the *instruments* by which Truth is apprehended. 4. The looking at the World with too *microscopic* an eye. These he discusses with much acuteness and logical power. . . . The speculations he occupies himself with are stated with quite as much verve as the subject is ever likely to command."—*The Examiner.*

LORD RANDOLPH CHURCHILL

A Study of
ENGLISH DEMOCRACY.

BY

JOHN BEATTIE CROZIER,

AUTHOR OF
'CIVILIZATION AND PROGRESS,' ETC.

LONDON:
SWAN SONNENSCHEIN, LOWREY & CO.
PATERNOSTER SQUARE.
1887.

Richard Clay & Sons,
Bread Street Hill, London,
Bungay, Suffolk.

CONTENTS.

CHAP.		PAGE
I.	INTRODUCTORY	1
II.	THE COGERS' HALL	12
III.	THE HOUSE OF COMMONS	36
IV.	THE RISE OF LORD RANDOLPH CHURCHILL	51
V.	LORD RANDOLPH CHURCHILL AS ORATOR	93
VI.	LORD RANDOLPH CHURCHILL AS STATESMAN	115
VII.	THE DANGERS OF ENGLISH DEMOCRACY	161
VIII.	THE PRESS AND THE DEMAGOGUE	189
IX.	THE ILLUSIONS OF THE PRESS	203

LORD RANDOLPH CHURCHILL.

CHAPTER I.

INTRODUCTORY.

I PROPOSE in the following pages to examine the political career of Lord Randolph Churchill, his principles, methods, and political aims; to take stock and inventory of the amount and quality of ability and character that have gone to make up his success; and more than all, to discover, if possible, the conditions at present existing in English Politics and Society, which have assisted or permitted such a man, with such intellectual and moral outfit, to rise to his present position of influence and power. In what I have to say I shall, I trust, maintain a perfectly neutral and disengaged attitude, avoiding all subjects of party controversy; I shall assume no political premises but such as may be admitted with equal readiness by Radical and Tory alike; and shall enunciate no political doctrines but such as may be held with equal sincerity by both.

In selecting Lord Randolph Churchill as a subject for study, I propose to regard him from a *political* rather than from a *personal* standpoint; for however interesting a man may be in himself, for political purposes no qualities however eminent will repay the trouble of investigation, unless the success they have brought to their possessor is an index and symbol of beliefs, prejudices, opinions, and modes of political judgment in the public mind;—of which indeed this very success is itself the product and outcome. Now did I believe that Lord Randolph Churchill had been thrust into power by aristocratic pressure, that his political rise and ultimate success were due entirely or even largely to the accident of birth, or were, as was the case formerly, the appanage of a particular family, I should have nothing to say. I should feel that the public had had no part in determining his career, that it might have witnessed his elevation without admiration, as it would have acquiesced in his degradation without censure, and accordingly I should pass him by unheeding. But it is because it is claimed for him by his admirers and a large section of the public, that his rise has been due almost entirely to his superiority in ability and character, that I am forbidden to pass him by; and that his career, by the light it throws on men's political judgments and modes of thought, is so pregnant with interest and instruction at the present time.

It has been so often repeated that it has almost passed into a truism, that the success of modern popular governments will depend largely on the kind of men in whom the People choose to repose confidence. However this may be, there can be little doubt that in such men, and especially in the circumstances of their rise, you may see what it is that the political public regard as ability, and what, for the time being at least, they regard as great and admirable. And, accordingly, believing as I do that in the rise of Lord Randolph Churchill you have imaged as in a mirror many if not all the vices, weaknesses, and illusions which still hang around the neck of Democracy and drag it down; and feeling the vast and supreme importance of this subject to all thinking minds (standing as we do still in the dawn of the new democracy), I have felt that my end would be best subserved by concentrating a steady light on this single prominent and representative figure, rather than by any merely general or abstract dissertation, however otherwise interesting or instructive. To avoid misunderstanding, however, I may as well perhaps say at once, that I have no fear of Democracy in itself; I am no political pessimist; and can contemplate the widest and most fundamental changes in the constitution of States unmoved, provided only that they are brought about with honest intent and with deliberate and well-grounded conviction. I have no sympathy with the perennial and ever-recurring cry of 'the State in danger;' nor do I share the fears of those who compare the approach of Democracy to the entrance on the Niagara rapids, and its advent to the shooting of the gulf; and as for the Demagogue, I know well that whatever else befalls the Democracy of the future, it will, like the good earth with its fungi and parasites, convert again into nutriment for itself such poor and imperfect instruments as from time to time it throws up to work out its purposes and minister to its designs. As for the old fear of

Despotism, the ghost of which is still so often raised to flutter the ignorant and weak-kneed, it has practically ceased to have any bearing on the future of the great majority of existing European States, and so far as we in England are concerned, it has almost entirely passed away. But there are nevertheless still certain defects bound up with all existing democracies—flaws inwoven in their texture—which are rather due to the age of the world and the stage of civilization reached at the present time, than inherent in the principle itself; and which in our own special form of democracy in England lie so close-hidden, so immediate to the very heart of the institutions from which we draw our political life, that in the clash and uproar of party strife, they have been almost entirely overlooked. These flaws and patches, like the wastes and morasses of the world, breed their own special and peculiar forms of life—forms which in rankness of growth, though not in body and fibre, often overtop the firmer and hardier products of the fields. Now it is in these swamps and watery wastes of the political world that are engendered and nourished careers like that of Lord Randolph Churchill, and out of which shoot and blow such reputations as those of which his is the supreme and topmost efflorescence.

As a diligent student of the relations existing between different kinds of political soil and the products that thrive on them, I have long been familiar with these unhealthy and noxious spots in our political system, and as I followed the course of public events with them in my mind, and observed the noble lord as a political seedling almost from his very inception and planting, I foresaw and even predicted his success from the outset; and when (his political fate having hung trembling in the balance for a moment while I hoped that my prediction might be falsified) his full-blown triumph at last justified my worst fears, I felt that such a blow had been given to all that intellectually and morally I had been taught to regard as great and honourable, as had not occurred in my time. As I watched the process from day to day, and saw the cheap expedients by which the whole business was accomplished; as I noticed the adaptation of the tree to the political compost on which it fed and out of which it grew, and saw the germs of notoriety reduplicating on themselves and blown into the general air till they filled the political sky, and his name became in every mouth a household word; I said to myself, not all the regiments of priests that patrol this land, with the innumerable bands of guerilla preachers at their back, will avail by their sweetest moral exhortation and appeal, to neutralize the deep temptation of this glittering career, or avert the steady gaze of young ambition from this blazing comet set in the sky for its imitation and worship. With this example ever before them, I asked myself, why should young political ability take the high and honourable road of tried and gradated service, waited on by the old English virtues of patience, moderation, and self-restraint, when it sees a licentious and unbridled tongue the shortest cut to the goal; when it has ocular proof before it that by the breach of all discipline and the casting aside of all those soft and restraining forms which alone make regulated and steady political action possible, you can so debauch and seduce the rabble and campfollowers, as at last to overcrow the General himself and alienate the common allegiance? And why, I still ask, waste the midnight oil over the laws of Political Economy and the deeper problems of States; why ransack History for the secret causes of the decline and fall of nations; or ponder over constitutions and codes, and their adjustments to circumstances of time and place; why travel in distant lands to mark the safeguards which wisdom and experience have devised to meet the shifts and preponderance of power; why, in a word, go into training for the higher qualities of the Statesman, when the supreme prize the Empire holds out to tried and experienced capacity, the very jewel of the Crown and service, can be snatched from its shelf by the first light and dexterous adventurer that passes by—in this case by one whose stock of ability, natural and acquired, for the higher requirements of Statesmanship, I pledge myself to show, before I have done, to be the slenderest and most shallow that have raised demagogue to power since the time when Cleon of Athens made the name a hissing and a byeword to men? Not that I for a moment dream, in saying this, that any words of mine or another's will avail to affect in the smallest degree the future and outlook of this once militant but now laurelled and triumphant politician.

There is a certain state of public sentiment (and you can feel it in the very air), when a reputation or notoriety once engendered, breeds in on itself in such multiple and ever-increasing ratio, that like those rabbit-warrens in Australia, or locust flights in Western America, the efforts of individuals to stay or arrest it are as impotent as to oppose the onward rolling sea. Nor can any merely political reverse or vicissitude do it; and in a state of public sentiment where political bribery leaves no personal stain, where the amusing political mountebank is as popular and safe from arrest as his brother of the music-hall and circus, and where, so long as party phrases are inviolate, political principles and even political allies may with impunity be whistled down the wind, there is not the slightest chance of it. I know of nothing that will do it, unless perchance it be a personal felony, an offence against the common law, the cheating at cards, or the suspicion of a *liaison* with a neighbour's wife. With the future career of the noble lord,* now complacently seated on the chair of State, I have no concern. I care not how in the future he may add to his stock of

* Autumn '86.

political knowledge, how he may change his tactics, trim his principles, or alter his political methods; nor shall I seek to anticipate (now that he has snatched the prize and is already showing signs of throwing away his cap and bells) the gravity and weight of public care with which his brows will be overhung—with all this I have no concern. But one thing I know, and that is, that whatever political fate await him, nothing can choke the strong conception of his rise under which I have groaned—and the many others, I trust, of whom for the time being I have ventured to make myself the mouthpiece. In taking up my pen therefore in this cause, it is not that I imagine that I can affect, nor do I wish to affect, his political future; nor would it avail anything if I could, for why try to uproot one political fungus when the political soil from which it has sprung continues to send up thousands more, if need be, to reproduce its kind? My only hope is that by setting him up as an illustration and example, I may strike at those fictions, illusions, and false political ideals which overrun and encumber the political field, and which have made it possible for ability such as this to climb to the topmost boughs of influence and power; and so, by gazetting once for all these blots and excrescences in our political system, to make, if possible, the attempt by another to play again the same game without detection, for his own political aggrandizement, difficult or impossible of success.

CHAPTER II.

THE COGERS' HALL.

SOME years ago, with the view of making clear to myself if possible the impressions made on miscellaneous popular assemblies by various types of oratory and public speaking, with the view too of defining more scientifically the form and type of political oratory that most easily and naturally bears sway over large representative assemblies, and especially the relation such type of ability bears to the real requirements and true qualities of statesmanship, I was in the habit of frequenting the rooms of a well-known debating society which held its meetings nightly in one of the old courts of Fleet Street, and which was, and I believe is still, known by the name of the Cogers' Hall. Lying as it did in the very centre of London, and in the immediate vicinity of the Temple and the great central offices of Literature and the Press, this well-known debating-room drew together in the course of a year a greater variety and range of talent perhaps than could elsewhere be met with; and not only by reason of the motley and ever-changing character of its audience, but from the variety of thought, style, and personality of the different speakers, furnished as just a mirror and epitome of public opinion as one could wish to find. The society, as I have already said, was an old one, and had held its debates night after night for a period far beyond living memory. "The subjects for discussion," as I have elsewhere described, "were usually the political and social topics of the hour, varied on rare occasions by light excursions into the region of religion, science, and philosophy. All sides of the political world were fairly represented; and if on one evening the Liberal, Radical, or Irish element in the room preponderated, on another, perhaps, the balance would incline to the High Tory or Conservative side. No restraint was put on the free expression of opinion, whether of applause or censure; so that the effect produced by the style, thought, or personality of the different speakers could be easily seen. The audience, too, was well adapted for purposes of observation, the circulation of fresh blood being constantly kept up; for, besides the old *habitués* who were a kind of constant quantity in the room, every evening brought in a fair contingent of casuals—passers-by who happened to read the subject of debate on the window outside and were attracted by curiosity to see what was going on, strangers from the country desirous merely of passing away the evening, or foreigners from various parts interested in politics and debate.

"The *personnel* of the room, too, was sufficiently varied and picturesque. Besides the ordinary Englishman of the middle class, who formed perhaps the staple of the meeting, there were to be seen in these rooms young barristers from the Temple, glowing with political or professional ambition, and come to cultivate the invaluable art of public speaking; hacks of the Press, broken down *littérateurs*, seedy Bohemians, with their coats out at elbow and driven to the wall by dissipation, who had dropped in to end the day over their pipes and punch, and who every now and then interrupted the debate by their confused, incoherent, or maudlin ejaculations; superior Working-men (with hair thrown back to bring out the intellect), who had gained praise and distinction, perhaps, among their own class in some local debating club in the suburbs, and who (although modestly deprecating their want of classical education) evidently rated themselves accordingly, and had come down to this central hall to try their prowess with the old veterans of debate. There, too, were to be seen Secularists of the Bradlaugh type, fed on Volney's *Ruins of Empires* and Paine's *Age of Reason*, who, with affected moderation of tone and studied reference to authorities, were prepared to demonstrate against all comers that kings and priests were the standing disgrace of the world, the long unmitigated curse of every nation and every age; brilliant young adventurers from Ireland, fresh from college and without any definite profession, who had come to London to push their fortunes, and were full of eloquence, fervour, and bright ingenuity; faded old book-worms, moths of the British Museum, who had come out quietly at night to this well-lit hall from its dusky recesses, where for years they had been collecting evidence to show that Julius Cæsar never existed, and that the ancient historians were impudent and unblushing forgeries of the Middle Ages;— all these were to be found here in this old hall on one or other evening, in hot but genial debate; and, with suffused and fiery-eyed demagogues screaming with excitement; Fenians, Socialists, and Red Republicans, threatening the general overturn of society without apology or disguise; old bachelors, city-clerks, half-pay captains, High Church curates, and occasionally some man well known in public life, come down to open a debate on the stirring question of the hour, made up as interesting and diversified an assemblage of characters as could well have been brought together.

"With an audience so varied, so shifting, and so rapid-changing in its composition, with debate untrammelled, and no restraint put upon a fair expression of feeling or opinion whether of applause or censure, the conditions needed for the observation of the effects of different forms and types of eloquence were peculiarly favourable. Nor, indeed, was the speaking less varied than the character and composition of the audience; but ranged through all stages of the good, bad, and indifferent. The most persistent and fatal type, perhaps, was the Bore—the old and well-seasoned bore—with good matter often, and sometimes ideas, but costive and speech-bound in utterance, whom nothing could kill or repress, who would wrestle with a platitude all night without remorse, and whose rising, by the ingenuities of torture with which it threatened the room, was the signal for a general stampede. A common type, too, was the ambitious Tyro who burned with some single idea, perhaps, which he could not repress, but who had not learned the art so well known to the old stagers, of making a single idea carry him with credit through a whole speech; and who, when he had polished and condensed his one idea into some weighty and audacious epigram (while the preceding speaker was addressing the room), and at last found his opportunity, rose and with rhetorical flourish fired it off with *éclat* and satisfaction; but having nothing further with which to follow it up, was left standing speechless, and so becoming confused, stammering, and, at last, hopelessly belated, sat down overwhelmed with confusion and shame. Then there was the Logic-chopper, with whom politics was a chain of syllogisms, and who insisted on wiredrawing each smallest platitude, and dividing it into its component parts, although the whole argument was of so thin, patent, and transparent a character that you could foresee his point, and have ample time to fall asleep, while he was winding his dreary and monotonous way among the successive links which he had interposed between his first premises and his ultimate conclusion. More tough and irrepressible, if not more wearisome, were the Hobbyists—the Anti-vaccination, Anti-vivisection, but particularly the Protection-hobbyist, who traced the decadence of England to her one-sided system of Free Trade, dragging it into every debate, and winding up invariably with the unanswerable poser, which he hurled as a Parthian shot at his opponents, 'What is the use of your cheap loaf if you have no Saturday night?' Of less frequent occurrence, but coming as it were from some higher atmosphere down to this worldly forum of debate, were to be seen the Idealist, young, soft, and of consumptive aspect, to whom this tough world offered no more difficulty for the construction of his airy dreams than if it were cobweb; the confirmed and unbending Moralist, who saw no reason why the millennium should not be realized now and here, if men would but follow the dictates of simple morality, and who would begin at once to inaugurate it by giving back Gibraltar to Spain, India to its own native population, and the blessings of 'home rule' and a 'constitution' to negroes, Zulus, Hottentots, and all the dwellers in the Southern Seas.

"The foregoing specimens, although typical and characteristic, were, most of them, loose and irrelevant in debate; but there were others deep in political knowledge, dangerous antagonists, who stuck to the subject in hand, going into matters elaborately; who came down to the rooms bristling with dry but pregnant and ugly statistics; men who knew the details of budgets, of exports and imports, of income-tax and legacy-duty, with the minuteness of an under-secretary to the Treasury; who could tell you the price of the quartern-loaf for each of the forty years preceding the repeal of the Corn Laws, and for each of the forty years since; who knew all about county government, rotten ships, and especially rotten boroughs, for which indeed they were prepared and armed with a complete scheme of grouping, redistribution, or extinction. Others again there were, whose memories were a complete *répertoire* of all the parliamentary debates of the last quarter of a century, men who knew what Lord Beaconsfield had said at the

Mansion House, or Lord Derby at Liverpool, and who, instead of meeting their opponents by direct arguments, pelted them indirectly with damaging phrases that at one time or another had fallen from their Parliamentary leaders; rolling under their tongues as if they were utterances of momentous import, such mystic and sublime phrases as 'peace with honour,' 'scientific frontier,' 'residuum,' 'Whigs bathing,' 'mending and ending,' 'plundering and blundering,' 'leaps and bounds,' 'extinct volcanoes,' and the like.

"Such were a few of the leading types of speakers who kept up the dreary hum and monotone of debate, and who, although in many cases exhibiting, in spite of defective utterance, genuine insight and common sense, made little or no impression on the room. But among the casual or habitual frequenters, there were always to be found one or more speakers of a different order, men, who although knowing little perhaps of the real difficulties of practical politics, and less of political detail, could by their brilliancy of handling, carry the room away over the heads of men of much more practical wisdom, business knowledge, and insight into the world and men." Now as I had observed that however much the audience changed in composition and character from night to night, these latter speakers maintained their popularity and supremacy undisputed throughout, it became my main concern to find out if possible what was the distinguishing feature in their speaking that gave them their pre-eminence amid all changes of audience and among men of all shades of thought and culture;—knowing well that if I could once succeed in seizing it, in insulating it, and in giving to it anything like firmness of outline and scientific precision, I should then be able (by comparing it with the type of intellect demanded for real statesmanship) to resolve the main question on which my mind was working, viz. :—What are the qualities which, in governments carried on by public discussion in large representative assemblies (like our own House of Commons), *naturally* rise to supremacy; and to what extent these qualities coincide with, or differ from, the qualities demanded for the best government of States?

Now owing as I have said to the great freedom of debate in these rooms, and to the full liberty that was accorded to all reasonable manifestations of applause or censure, you could, after watching for a time the effect produced by the different speakers on the various changes of audience, forecast almost to a certainty from the style alone of the speakers, irrespective of their matter, the permanent estimation in which they would be held by the room, and the permanent level of prestige to which they would attain. And as the relative ranking of the different speakers was not a mere individual or private estimate, but was usually the solid opinion of the whole room, you could as easily have predicted, had the audience been called on to form a Cabinet, who would have been chosen as Prime Minister on either side, and who as chief lieutenants and subordinates, as you could the selection of a representative team of cricketers from a large and varied collection of the best known players. And the longer I sat in these rooms, the more increasingly clear did it become to me, that in popular political assemblies men, if left to themselves, take grade and ranking not at all, as might be expected, in proportion to the real depth, complexity, and extent of their knowledge of the subject in hand, nor yet of their knowledge and judgment in general, but rather in proportion to their possession of certain extrinsic, irrelevant, and more or less *ad captandum* qualities, which are as often to be found united with shallowness and superficiality as with real depth and insight. A speaker, for example, might have a deep knowledge of the question in hand, and of course the more of it the better; a clear and connected, even if more or less flimsy, thread of argument he must have; and, the debates being serious, a certain show at least of earnestness and conviction too was indispensable; but the distinctive feature, the feature that gave rank and eminence to the debaters, was the power of brilliant personal characterization, conveyed in a metaphorical and glowing, and above all in a rapid flowing style —a power I have remarked which seems to be so level with, and so accurately adapted, pitched, and attuned to the great ruling illusions, admirations, and ideals of the average human mind, cultured and uncultured alike, as to impress it, when the opportunity offers, more than aught else besides, and to seem synonymous with ability or genius itself. A man might show himself to be an excellent debater, so far as practical judgment and knowledge of the question in hand were concerned, whether in principle or in detail; he might see clearly the causal relations and connexions of the facts with which he was dealing, and abound in statistics, facts, and figures having an intimate bearing on the subject under discussion; but if he happened to be slow, constrained, and hesitating in speech, or delivered himself in a cold, dry, or uninteresting manner, he would make little or no impression on the bulk of the audience, and the room after listening for a time with apathy or weariness, would, if his speech were prolonged, begin slowly to empty itself. One man in particular I remember whose speeches gave me personally more real insight into what I myself wanted to know in order to arrive at a sound judgment on the many questions that came under discussion than those of any one else in the room, but owing to his somewhat irregular, spasmodic, and speech-bound style and manner, all his fine points did him but little service with the audience, and were speedily neutralized or spirited away by the swoop of some light and facile Bohemian, perhaps, who would follow him in the debate, and who, instead of dealing directly with the political facts and their meanings and connexions, would, by giving the debate a personal turn, by personal invective or light and easy banter, by cunningly diverting the audience to the style and peculiarities of his opponent, or by assuming a high superiority of view, and gratuitously characterizing his method of argument as pedantic, pettifogging, or worthy of a vestryman, steal away the admiration and suffrages of the room. Indeed this trick of starting a personal diversion when the subject was dry, or your knowledge of it was scanty, was a favourite one with the more alert and brilliant speakers (more especially when they were conscious of lack of matter), and never failed, to my remembrance, when brilliantly and dexterously executed, and when judiciously intermingled with a show of earnestness and logical coherence, to impress the room with a vague but none the less potent impression of the speaker's general intellectual superiority.

Now, as a man may have a clean-cut image of a complicated subject in all its bearings and relations, and yet from want of practice or original power of expression may be unable to do justice to his knowledge in a speech, and so fail to convince and persuade a popular audience, it is evident that the supremacy accorded in popular debating assemblies to the brilliant, rapid, flashing *littérateur* over the man of wise, practical, and solid judgment, can only be possible in subjects where the truth or untruth of different opinions cannot be brought to any immediate, practical, or decisive test. Were the problem to be solved, for example, one in mathematics, or in physics, astronomy, or practical medicine, where the sight and demonstration of the truth can be made to follow close on the heels of the hypothesis raised, all this superficial verbal decoration which under other circumstances is so attractive, all these pleasing and titillating personalities, these strokes of caustic humour which the stream of eloquent speech bears along with it, and which emblazon its rich and flowing robe with metaphors as with jewels, would be felt to be an impertinence, glamour, or evasion, and would be resented as such; and provided only the speaker could give us assurance that the truth was being evolved like the statue out of the marble, and that each blow or stroke of thought was bringing us a step nearer to it, he might go on stumbling and stammering all along the line of his discourse (as I have heard done) without serious detriment to his reputation or authority. But in Practical Politics, where (the complex nature of Man having to be dealt with) the effect of any proposal, however simple, is at best more or less a matter of speculation only; where your opinion right or wrong cannot (and this is the fatal circumstance) be verified or refuted in the sight of gods and men, but must await the dilatory lapse of time; where even the wisest judgment must often at points, instead of touching solid ground, swim on a sea of probability and hypothesis merely; and where one man's opinion being regarded as as good as another's, all are considered more or less shaky and uncertain; a speaker's reputation and authority will depend rather on his *mode of handling* the question, than on the real depth of his insight into it, and will turn chiefly on the skilful use he makes of all those pleasing and decorative arts, those airy personalities, metaphorical allusions, pictorial bye-play and quotation, which although they often, like personal beauty, tend to falsify the issue rather than to irradiate it, nevertheless by certain laws of the mind leave the impression of general and all round superiority and power. Nor, indeed, if we search for these laws shall we fail in discovering them. Truth, absolute Truth, is, if I may say so, the supreme goddess of man (as Belief, its counterpart in the mind, is his most powerful spring of action), and when she is in presence, all lesser deities shrink abashed away; but in her absence flights of inferior spirits issue from their hiding-places, and by the illusions which they create, as in a fairy dream, become for the time being all-powerful. These rapid and tricksy turns of allusion, metaphor, personality, quotation, wit and fancy, by their spontaneity and the impossibility there is of predicting their impact or the direction of their flight, interest and arouse the imagination on their own account; and whatever arouses the imagination, by that fact alone has communicated to it a sense of unknown charm and illimitability. And just as when the absolute truth about a man or woman cannot be known, personal beauty, as being the *natural* expression of an internal and hidden beauty, carries with it great weight by the charm which it produces, and as, alas! too often happens, encourages an easy and fatal credence to a corresponding beauty of character, which, however, in real life need not exist; so, in Politics, where no demonstration is forthcoming, where truth is not in visible presence and cannot be had for the asking, and where time alone can test the value of opinion, the dazzling arts and graces of the orator or phrasemonger are sure by their stimulus to the imagination to prevail, unless indeed we are armed and on our guard against them, and this for the simple reason that when genuine they have, like Beauty, their roots deep down in the heart of man, and like it are the clothing and vesture with which Nature endows a full and various, a refined or beautiful mind.

Now this tendency in popular political assemblies, whether cultured or uncultured, to select men as leaders rather for their *mode of handling* a question than for their *real judgment and insight* into it, was the first important truth that established itself to my own satisfaction, and with something like scientific precision, at the old Cogers' Hall; and now that we have ourselves entered on the reign of Democracy, where the all-important point in success is the choice of good leaders, the knowledge of this law of popular assemblies, by keeping the judgment awake to one of the main sources of illusion by which it is dazzled and deflected, will be seen to be in its bearings and significance of cardinal and indeed world-wide importance.

The second great truth which I learned at these old discussion rooms—a truth allied to the first, and one which from its wide applicability to life, and especially from its bearing on our judgments of men and the illusions against which we have to guard in our estimate of them, is also of first and cardinal importance—was this, viz. that men take rank in public estimation according to the side at which they are viewed, so that the same man shall show brilliant or dull, shall be voted a genius or a bore, according to the *angle* at which he chooses to present himself for judgment or estimate. If you take, for example, a number of practical business men, and set them down around a table with a view to their deliberating on some public or private course of action or conduct, you will find that (as mere empty declamation or rhetoric would be entirely out of place around a table) the man among them who will most clearly seize the point on which the business in hand hinges, no matter how slow and hesitating his utterance may be, will be awarded the place of honour—

his imperfect powers of expression not derogating in the least from his position of power or authority; but if you put the same men through the ordeal of explaining, elaborating, and enforcing their views before a popular assembly, the chances are that the light, nimble, and vivacious talker among them, the one who by mere rhetoric and the manipulation of phrases can make the worse appear the better reason, will bear away the palm. Here is a great mathematician, for example, a great scientist, a great theologian, physician, or even a great chess-player, men who if you set them down before the great problems that are to be solved in their various lines of thought, will by the width and extent of their knowledge, their depth, farsightedness, and comprehension of view, tower away over all competitors ; but if you will insist that they shall make good their superiority before a popular audience by *speech* alone (especially if you cannot bring the matter to a decisive and convincing test) in the face of a number of superficial and hostile wits and sciolists, the chances are that your great men will be out of the running altogether. So great a difference does it make to the repute in which you are held in this world, whether you have to exhibit your talents under conditions where, as around a small table, pure insight and power of thought alone tell, and are alone available, or whether you have to exhibit them before a large assembly where fluency and rapidity of speech, and the arts and graces of rhetoric and illusion, can so dazzle and perplex the issue as to obscure the truth. I have known ranters who, appearing before a hard-headed political gathering, disgusted them by their merely sentimental appeals, and were voted of no weight or consequence, but who would carry all before them with ease at a temperance society, a mother's meeting, or with a religious and fanatic mob. Humorists again you will have noticed who are at their exact and proper angle in an after-dinner speech, and can with ease and grace keep the table in a roar, but who quite lose their wits, their very sense of humour forsaking them, when they have to give their minds to the connected links of thought and argument involved in a long and serious debate. It is not uncommon to find that the very men who when criticizing the schemes of others are masters of personal invective, when set down to construct a scheme of their own are impotent or lost.

The most brilliant, polished, and splendid speaker I have ever known was in his private conversation so wanting in form, his tone and bearing were so loose and familiar, so wanting in dignity, simplicity, and reserve, that, to those who did not know him as an orator, he left almost invariably the impression (quite unjustly too) of insincerity, cheapness, and worse than all of commonness. On the other hand, again, it is a common observation that gentlemen (often of the aristocracy) whose personal manners are impressive and dignified, who have a high tone, and bear about with them an air of distinction, whose personal and private observations, too, are marked by great good-sense, propriety, and measure, when they rise to address a popular audience, find themselves at so false and unaccustomed an angle for the exhibition of their proper merits, that they seem quite to lose all their impressiveness, and end by leaving on the audience a sense only of boredom or stupidity. I have heard at one time or another most of the great Thinkers, Scientists, Theologians, and Publicists of the day addressing public audiences, and so poor at best are they as mere public speakers that, I can confidently testify, if they appeared unknown and unrecognized before an audience at the Cogers' Hall, each and all of them with scarcely an exception would, if he spoke extemporaneously, weary if not empty the room. So strange is it, and yet so true, that were there no other medium for the communication of thought but the public platform, the greatest intellects of the day would have to bend, if it came to the popular vote, before the over-blown phrasemongers, pulpit-orators, and demagogues of the hour, following in their train and gracing their victorious procession as captive kings in a Roman triumph.

So important is it that we should see these things (if in our judgment of men from the angle at which they happen to present themselves we are not to be swamped and sunk in illusion), that I consider these two great truths which I learned at the Cogers' Hall, and reduced there almost to a scientific certainty, have, in the age of Democracy which is now come upon us, alone more than repaid me for the many hours which I sometimes thought I was wasting, as I sat a silent listener night after night in these old discussion rooms. Carrying then with us these two great truths—first, that in this world men take rank and position according to the *angle* from which they are viewed; and secondly, that the talents that give supremacy (and are at their proper angle) in representative political assemblies, are not, like the talents that give supremacy around a council table, the true qualities of knowledge, judgment, and practical wisdom that are required in the wise government of States— as torches against darkness, and charms against enchantment or illusion, we will now proceed by their light and protection to trace the political career of Lord Randolph Churchill, and to note, without dazzle or bewilderment, the successive steps by which he has attained to his present position of authority and power. But first a word or two on the House of Commons.

CHAPTER III.

THE HOUSE OF COMMONS.

In the last chapter I endeavoured to indicate the type and quality of public speaking which gave pre-eminence and *prestige* under the entirely free and natural conditions of debate, as it was carried on in the old discussion rooms off Fleet Street. With the view of still further testing, as it were, by a kind of crucial experiment, how far the same qualities bore sway under less free and spontaneous conditions, I was in the habit, during the period I am describing, of going down to the House of Commons for an hour or two in the evening, not only on the occasion of important debates, but during its ordinary sittings. Here I found, as I had expected, that great deductions would have to be made, and many complex considerations taken into account, before the normal effects of different kinds of oratory and debating power could be clearly and distinctly seen.

In the Cogers' Hall, there being, as we have seen, little or no restraint imposed on the audience in their manifestations of applause or censure, if a speaker bored the room he was promptly and peremptorily 'roughed' down. In the House of Commons, on the other hand, members being there rather in a representative than in an individual or personal capacity, they could not, if they became wearisome, be treated quite so unceremoniously; and in consequence might often be seen stretched over the House like a pall through long regions of the night. At the Cogers' Hall, again, there were no momentous issues hanging on the results of debate to cloud the brow; no constituents lying at the speaker's back like menacing shadows to warn him off dangerous or uncertain courses; wealth and birth gave no distinction or advantage; there were no great prizes of office at stake; and as the room was constantly changing in composition and character, neither fear of consequences, traditional respect for individuals, nor deference to customary forms or established reputations, interfered to disguise one's perception of the oratorical or debating qualities that were at heart most admired. It might therefore fairly be claimed that the type and quality of speaker who maintained his supremacy through all changes of audience, was a very accurate measure and index of the type and quality of speaker who under free and spontaneous conditions would rise to supremacy anywhere. But in the House of Commons all this was changed. Far from being the democratic assembly where personal merit alone prevailed, and where men took rank and status purely according to the exhibition of personal ability or power, it was still largely aristocratic in temper, tone, and habits of thought; wealth and birth still counted for much, and in the race for office, gave high and various points of vantage. Models of public speaking, too, had long become stereotyped; many of the members had long been invested with all the halo that comes from age, genius, or *prestige;* important debates were apt to end in practical action involving grave consequences to the lives and fortunes of many; and behind all, the constituencies stood like sentinels, with bayonets fixed, in the shadowy background. Opinion being thus handicapped in so many different directions, the difficulty in determining the type of public speaking that was most admired, and which, if an opening presented itself, would naturally rise to supremacy and power, was much increased. One common feature, however, it was curious and interesting to note by the way, amid these many different conditions presented by the two places, and that was that the same old types of speakers that we saw at the Cogers' Hall reproduced themselves here in all their ancient picturesqueness and variety. Here too was the old bore—the impenetrable, pachydermatous bore—who had neither matter nor manner, and who made frantic efforts to deliver himself but in vain; the young and nervous but ambitious beginner with one idea, which he hastened to sow all at once like a whirlwind and then collapsed; the tedious and fretful logic-chopper, whose steps were so slow and painful that you could fall asleep between them and miss nothing of importance; the Hobbyists —anti-Vaccination, anti-Vivisection, anti-Contagious Diseases Act, but chiefly Protectionist— who shot their hobbies at their antagonists like bolts before they sat down; the idealists, the enthusiasts, the high attenuated moralists, the peace-at-any-price men. Here were also the genial and kindly humourists, the specialists, the platitudinarians, the pessimists, the quoters from other men's speeches, and the masters of statistics and detail. Here they all were in their naked reality, humming and hawing, stuttering and shuffling and stumbling as I had seen their prototypes in Fleet Street—and before the reporters in the gallery had trimmed, clean-shaved, and made them respectable for the morning papers. So like indeed in style, manner, and delivery was the average member of the House to the average Coger, so similar was the impression that he produced on the mind, and so like was he in the handling of the questions that came before him, that you had only to close your eyes during a debate and listen, and you would imagine yourself back again in the old rooms. The bulk of honourable members had evidently made a wide and extensive study of the subjects to which they had given their attention; but so over-freighted were they with stolidity and phlegm, that they were unable to give to their ideas anything like rapid, brilliant, or effective utterance; and depended rather, for the painting out and expression of their finer shades of meaning, on emphasis and gesticulation than on speech; and when they did succeed in preserving the appearance of smoothness (and getting time as well for fore-thought), it was by the mechanical repetition at the beginning of each sentence of the concluding words or clauses of the last. And yet they kept their eyes in great measure well on the practical issues and concrete bearings of their subject, and concealed beneath their stolidity a large measure of good sense and sobriety of thought. The only type of speaker I missed from the House of Commons (but now that the suffrage is extended I do not expect we shall have to wait for him long) was the ranter—the seething and foaming ranter—whose words, which were of the cheapest newspaper quality, ran like a watery flux, but like shadows left no abiding image in the mind, and disclosed behind them neither grasp, power, nor hold on reality.

Such was the House of Commons before, and indeed since, the last extension of the suffrage; and in spite of the important issues hanging on its debates, and the good sense and practical knowledge they exhibited, when one remembered by contrast some of the great nights at the Cogers' Hall, when party feeling ran high on some sore or exciting topic of the hour, and when one recalled the rapid, brilliant assaults of the leaders of the opposing forces with their concentrated fire of eloquence, invective, quotation and personality, all playing around one's head like forked lightning, one was bound to confess that a night at the House of Commons, except perhaps on the most momentous occasions (and even these as mere oratorical displays were pale and colourless in comparison), was such a bore and weariness as was not elsewhere to be met with. I remember taking a friend with me to the House one evening on the occasion of an important debate in which many of the best speakers were engaged, and on our leaving somewhat wearied, my friend, who had been in the habit of going with me at times to the rooms off Fleet Street, burst on me in a tone of mingled surprise and disappointment by observing that in his opinion not one of these distinguished members whose names were known over the wide world could be fairly ranked higher as a mere speaker, than what he was pleased to call a 'second-rate Coger.' And, although I myself felt, and had long before perceived, that, so far as mere oratorical power was concerned, his remark was perfectly just and true, I nevertheless felt bound to remind him that members were elected and sent to the House of Commons, in the great majority of cases, not for their oratorical powers at all, but as practical and trustworthy men to manage the affairs and business of the nation; and that it was unreasonable and even absurd to expect, as the public apparently did, that these men—business men past middle life who had not been accustomed to cultivate the arts of speech or produce their knowledge at their tongue's tip at a moment's notice, or country gentlemen who by their position and training would but for the necessities of debate be naturally inclined to despise these accomplishments—should be as amusing and as brilliant, as mere speakers, as young men with a natural genius for oratory who had gravitated to the public discussion rooms from the wide waste of natural talent drifting about the London streets. And furthermore, that it was equally absurd to expect that debates which were to end in some course of practical action often affecting seriously the lives and fortunes of men, and which in consequence were weighted down to the ground by documents, statistics, reports, figures, and other tedious and wing-clipping technicalities and detail, should rise to the same easy flights of rhetoric and fancy, and be as amusing to listen to, as mere rhetorical exercises which had the boundless air wherein to execute their ideal sweep, unclogged by earthly detail, and which could sail along the wind without ballast of personal responsibility or rudder of definite goal. But my friend who had been born and brought up under the supposition that the Statesman and the Orator were one, was disillusioned notwithstanding, and went away bereaved. The truth is, the reputation of the House of Commons for oratory as such is a mere fiction, an illusion of the public mind which has been accustomed to associate the names of great statesmen with great orators—Burke, Chatham, Pitt, Fox, and the rest—and so by habit has come to imagine statesmanship and oratory to be more or less synonymous. And this illusion has been seconded and reflected by the Press, and this for two reasons;—first, in a general way, with the object of keeping up the public confidence in statesmen as such, which without some quality which could be held up prominently for admiration would be apt to flag; and secondly, in special instances, for Party purposes, and in order to give the requisite outfit, finish, and completeness to party leaders or party men, whom for other reasons it is desirable to aggrandize and invest with the qualities which the public from long habit have been accustomed to expect. And yet in spite of the fact that members are not returned on account of their possession of the qualities that go to make up the brilliant talker, or to do work for which mere speech however brilliant is best adapted, as I sat listening to these debates and observed (as the dreary waste of speech dragged its slow length along) what a relief and godsend any little audacity, impertinency, or joke was to the bored and jaded honourable member; how highly a little personal satire, mild banter, or even third-rate metaphor was appreciated by him; as I witnessed the laughter and applause that arose over a piece of coarse but perhaps pungent invective; I said to myself, were a few men of real rapidity, brilliancy, lightness of touch, and power of personal characterization (even if their real knowledge of public business and affairs were merely nominal), men of such qualities as I remembered in one or two brilliant instances in the old debating rooms, to be let down into the House of

Commons in the democratic days that are now coming over it, they would as surely, if more slowly, rise to pre-eminence and power there, as they did at the old Cogers' Hall. I am not forgetful of course of the old sneer that men are soon made to find their level in the House of Commons—a sneer which expressed a sufficient truth at a time when the men of *birth* who ruled were able to put down the men of mere *talent* (at whom alone you will observe the sneer is usually levelled) who might have disputed their supremacy. At the time of Burke, for example, when the aristocracy reigned alone and supreme in the Commons, men were said to find their level there, and so indeed it proved to be; for so heavily did they bear on him with their whole weight that he was never able to rise to a seat in the Cabinet. During the Middle-class *régime*, again, of the last fifty years, when the *Times* made the sneer seem a truism by the persistency with which it hurled it at great Thinkers and writers, John Stuart Mill, whom not only the ordinary member but Cabinet ministers *now* quote as if he were a kind of political pope, was made to find his level in the House by having his political opinions more or less generally ignored. The phrase might indeed have been used, and with as little sense, of Shakspeare himself, who owing to his lowly birth and position was regarded by the kings and lords of his day as of so little account that he was allowed to find his natural level by living and dying almost entirely unknown and unrecorded. 'Tis a poor superstition this, and one not yet exploded, of men finding their level in the House of Commons, and it may be predicted that now that Democracy is here, and the Aristocracy and Plutocracy combined can no longer by themselves alone countervail the influence of men of talent, this purse-proud sneer will work in the opposite and inverse direction; and instead of the wonder being that a man like Burke was not allowed to rise to a seat in the Cabinet, the wonder will be that men with the qualities of wisdom, knowledge, and far-sightedness which go to make up real statesmanship, will be displaced by qualities which are more nearly at the right angle for success in popular assemblies, viz. the qualities of the first-class 'Coger.' All lines of observation and thought indeed lead up to this, and even now, when I look around for the make-weights and compensating checks which are to prevent such a consummation, I confess I am not able to find them. The Prime Minister for the time being, as we see, recruits his Cabinet largely from men possessed of this class of ability, making as they do the most showy and effective skirmishers for attack or defence; and they in turn by the mere lapse of time gradually succeed, as was the case with Lord Beaconsfield, in the reversion to the leadership. The average Member of Parliament again (like the motley and ever-changing throng that from first to last I saw pass in and out of the old discussion rooms), if you will listen carefully to his expressed estimates of men, regards this class of ability as synonymous with genius itself, and bends before it as before a natural superiority—always premising that the jokes, sarcasms, personalities, and 'happy phrases' are addressed to the House itself by honourable members, and are not the mere cuttings from a penny newspaper—the offspring perhaps of the brain of some poor hack out at elbows. And lastly, the Press, which is mainly if not wholly instrumental, in the first instance at least, in giving members of Parliament their rank and *prestige* in the country, is, as I shall show further on, equally under the dominion of this idea; but even were it not so, it is so bound up with Party Politics that its individual organs, from the *Times* downwards, are forced to take advantage of every form of ability however flimsy that finds favour with the great masses of voters, in order to strengthen and reinforce themselves against their opponents. Whichever way we look, therefore, all the influences, currents, and winds of opinion that sweep through the Democratic Era on which we are now entering, make for the aggrandizement of the Talker, the Phrase-monger, the Demagogue, and tend, as we shall see more clearly further on, to accelerate rather than retard his rise.

Such were the observations and reflections I carried away with me from the House of Commons, and when, not long after when I had ceased my attendance there, the name of Lord Randolph Churchill began to attract attention, and became familiar to me through the space he occupied in the Press, it occurred to me, with what truth we shall afterwards see, that here possibly was a man of the type of ability that I had been looking for in the House of Commons, and who, I had predicted, would, if he made his appearance there, soon make for himself a distinguished mark and position.

In my next chapter therefore I propose to trace the rise of Lord Randolph Churchill, and to follow the connection and interaction of the causes and influences that have lifted him to his present position of influence and power.

CHAPTER IV.

THE RISE OF LORD RANDOLPH CHURCHILL.

LORD RANDOLPH CHURCHILL was already past thirty years of age, and had sat in the House of Commons for some six or seven years, taking little or no part in debate, when the general public were first made aware of his existence by his procedure in the Bradlaugh debates, when he and a few other malcontents openly mutinied against their leader, and formed a Cave under the designation of 'the Fourth Party.' After seven years of unexampled power and prosperity the Conservatives had been thoroughly defeated at the recent elections, and on returning to the House were to be seen sitting nightly, like mourners at a funeral service, on their thinned and empty benches, speechless, drooping, and altogether broken in spirits. Not that there was anything unusual in this sudden reversal at the polls; on the contrary, it was quite within the normal course of party politics; and with a little vigilance and patience on the part of the Conservatives, opportunities would soon again have presented themselves for routing their opponents in the open field, and in fair and honourable debate. But as the memory of their long prosperity fell athwart the gloom of their present fortunes, it brought with it a feeling of discontent, discontent in turn engendered restlessness and impatience, and all combined moved them to seek a present consolation by casting a darkening shade on their high-minded and chivalrous leader, who was felt to be too 'slow,' and to have too little 'go,' to stem the hot and pent-up tide of long-delayed but now triumphant Liberalism. The mutineers of the Fourth Party who shared this latent and diffused feeling more largely perhaps than others, and from a variety of causes fretted under it with more impatience, were the first to give expression to it by casting off the authority of their official leader publicly and without disguise, and betaking themselves to the open country, where, like a gang of gipsy bandits who had thrown off the soft and restraining forms of civilized warfare, they were prepared to carry on a kind of desultory Ishmaelitish struggle, their hands against every man's, and where, like a band of Choctaw Indians, they could come to scalps without formality, neither giving nor receiving quarter. Holding as they did that the main function of an Opposition was to oppose, rightly or wrongly, instead of giving spirit and life to that opposition by bringing to the great topics of debate a greater brilliancy of handling, or a wider range and sweep of thought, they sought rather to gain their ends by arts more adapted to their powers—the meaner and baser arts of obstruction, exaggeration, and personal abuse. Instead of a finer and more central characterization of men or measures, they relied on the cheap tricks of the caricaturist and sign-painter; for substantial argument they substituted abusive personalities; and instead of turning aside the stream of hostile legislation by greater agility, subtlety, or power, they blocked it bodily by great boulders of mechanical obstruction. They might have been seen night after night when any Bill of great reach and importance was before the House, sitting over it like cats over rat-holes, ready to strangle each detail the moment it emerged, while in the meantime the great principle and scope of the Bill (of which these petty details were but incidents), like some great mammal, passed by unheeded; and this proceeding, which gave them a show of industry and zeal, was characterized by them and their partizans as a 'fighting of the measure clause by clause.' So essentially poor and mean (although useful, as the event has proved to themselves) were their tactics, so insignificant were their personal powers, and so long had the spirit in which they conducted debate been outgrown in all civilized assemblies, that had each of the party gone on his own way separately from the others, voting as he pleased, acting as he pleased, speaking as he pleased, in all probability nothing more would have been heard of them. But by formally and deliberately cutting themselves off from the general leadership and forming a separate camp within the borders of their own party; by assuming for themselves and policy a distinctive name and title; and by choosing for themselves a leader; they excited in the House a degree of curiosity and interest that would otherwise have been denied them. And as all this was enacted on the high and imperial stage of the House of Commons, to be seen of every eye and

blown by the Press to the four corners of
the world, it gave to these political seedlings
in their germ and inception just that amount
of flutter, titillation, and interest in the popular
imagination which was so necessary and indeed indispensable to their personal designs.
In the House itself, where their insignificance,
their unscrupulousness, and their levity were
most apparent, they were regarded as objects
of curiosity and speculation rather than of
anxiety or fear. But into the dignity, decorum,
and, it must be added, mortal dulness of debate
they let in the new and more lively elements of
familiarity, buffoonery, and personal abuse—
elements which, however much in the end, like
punning, destructive of all serious debate, for
the time being gave the appearance of greater
life, vivacity, and 'go'; and Lord Randolph
Churchill as being at once the youngest, the
most irrepressible, and most abusive, drew to
himself the largest share of interest and attention. Not knowing at any moment the curve he
was likely to take, or the character and pose he
was likely to assume, his movements by reason
of this very uncertainty were watched with as
much interest, and excited as much curiosity,

as those of the Prime Minister himself. What with his rank, his reputation for youth, his transparent but studied insolence; what with the free and ambi-dextrous way in which he struck out on all sides of him, and the levity with which he relieved and lightened it all; he enjoyed the rare felicity of being petted in turn by each of the parties whom he in turn supported, without exciting the alarm of any; while his political insignificance, and the derisive laughter he evoked when each in turn became the target for his vituperation, shielded him from their malice and resentment. He was not, in a word, regarded as a serious politician, or indeed as a politician at all; but was looked on, as was natural from his procedure, as a spoilt child, to be petted and caressed rather than coerced; or rather perhaps as a mischief-making antic retained on the premises for the entertainment and amusement of the House. Imbued with this feeling, which indeed was general among honourable members, and little recking of the dangerous nature they were warming to their bosom, the leading men on both sides amused themselves immensely with his diversions, and by their countenance encouraged him in what they regarded as after all mere freaks of naughtiness or whim. The rank and file of both parties did the same. The long rows of Squires, in particular, who sat more or less speechless themselves behind the front Conservative Bench, who were too indolent to trouble themselves seriously with the conduct and *morale* of their party, and who sat or lounged there night after night, dry and bored, awaiting the dinner-hour,—gentlemen who were themselves too deeply imbued with the old spirit of parliamentary courtesy to strike at their opponents 'below the belt,' but who naturally hated the Government and all its works (now that their dearest privileges were beginning to be attacked) with the mortal hatred of men fighting for their lives,—were secretly delighted to have found an instrument who under the guise of youth and recklessness had no such scruples, and cheered in consequence his most coarse and heartless strokes till the roof rang with the echoes of their applause.

The Liberal members, on the other hand, while immensely enjoying the insolence with which he flouted his own leaders, regarded these stabs and thrusts at theirs as but the sham and mock-heroic outbursts of an over-flattered impotence, as the ravings of some moon-struck envious comedian practising the part of heavy tragedy before the glass, but with the lines of low comedy all too deeply ingrained to be erased; and joined accordingly their shouts of derisive laughter to the chorus of Opposition applause. So entertaining indeed did he become all round, and so much 'go,' as it was called, did he give to the dreary routine of debate by these irrelevant and even vulgar personalities, that the House, which could scarcely keep together a sufficient number of members at the dinner hour for the transaction of serious public business (unless, indeed, on questions of urgent and momentous importance), would witness them trooping in, night after night, in great numbers, to enjoy the sight of this versatile comedian—now as a little gladiator putting on and off his sword, now as a merry-andrew changing his cap and bells, now indulging in idle horse-play like a rustic at a village fair. And this too when he was already over thirty years of age, and had sat in Parliament for the greater part of a decade! Had he indeed literally as well as metaphorically come down to the House with his sword, drawn it on the open floor, and, like Mark Antony after the battle of Actium, challenged the Prime Minister to mortal combat, he could not have been taken less seriously —except occasionally, perhaps, by the Prime Minister himself. As it was, I am convinced that had the debates been more or less private, as in the time of Pitt, and he and his diversions been left in consequence to be dealt with by the House itself, he would have remained to this day, as I shall show further on, a mere appanage to the establishment, to be brought in and out as occasion served to relieve the tedium and monotony of debate. But there were two great forces in operation — forces which, however right, necessary, and indeed inseparable from our present stage of civilization and development, will, if a man is so fortunate as to be caught in their sweep and current, like the rise of eunuchs in the Byzantine Empire, carry him on to fortune and power, not so much by his glory as by his shame. These forces are the power of the Public Press, and the operation of the system of Party Politics.

The Press, whose public function in a democratic age is, as I shall hereafter show, to stand as a winnowing-fan or disinfecting sheet between Parliament and the People, to prevent the passage of germs of morbid or unhealthy notoriety into the general air, there to infect and poison the minds of men; which should have a care that none but qualities of real statesmanship should by mere reverberation and repetition have a chance of fastening themselves on the public imagination, but should ruthlessly insulate and destroy all morbid activities in their very inception; the Press, I say, whose public function is this or it is nothing, finding that the procedure of Lord Randolph Churchill had become an object of interest and curiosity out of doors, and that a record of his personal scurrilities enlivened the dreary columns of debate provided for consumption at the morning breakfast-table, took almost from the very beginning to reporting his impertinences, buffooneries, and exaggerations at full length and in large saturating doses, bestowing as much space and comment on them as on the details of a divorce suit, a prize-fight, or a trial for murder. In thus sending up his name like an air-balloon in the gaze of the gaping world, and blowing it around the pendant globe to be seen of every eye (the first thing that met you in the morning on the placards was most likely to be in staring type, 'Scene in the House of Commoms—Lord R. Churchill and Mr. Gladstone'), the Press stamped him deeply into the public imagination from the very beginning, and gave him at his very birth as a politician more importance and consequence than the founders of most religions have received at their death. Nor would this have been surprising had they believed they had discovered in him any hidden germs of real statesmanship. On the contrary, they regarded him from the beginning (and I appeal to the memory of my readers in support of this) as an impertinent vulgar lampooner and buffoon; they spoke of him habitually as a political Puck; the Comic Illustrated Papers especially reflecting the prevailing opinion by picturing him at one time as a little merry-andrew amusing the House with his cap and bells; at another, as a sulky, brazen-eyed, self-important pug; and again, as an unfortunate cur let loose on the Derby course with a tin-kettle tied to its tail for the amusement of the crowd.

Now it was about this time (say a year or two after his first appearance) that, interested to learn what style or quality of speaker and debater he was, and with my old experience of the Cogers' Hall at my back as a kind of metre or standard of judgment, I determined to go down to the House and hear him for myself. And reserving details of what I have to say of him as a public speaker until the next chapter, I may be permitted to observe here in passing, that when, to my disgust, I found the object of all this public interest and attention popping up at every angle and pause in debate, and in the most insolent, frivolous, and, worse than all, palpably vulgar and insincere manner wasting the time of the House with his irrelevant, irritating, and trivial questions, and amusing or disgusting it with his abusive personalities; and all too, to my surprise, on a range and scale of speaking ability which I can testify would have shamed a third-rate 'Coger'; and when I remembered the real wealth of speaking and debating ability that could on any night be had (out at elbows) in the old discussion-room for a pot of ale; when I thought of all this, I said to myself, Here is a man who, merely because he acts on the exalted stage of the House of Commons, where he is seen of all the world, and the Press carries his every word to the ends of the earth, threatens, by the interest which his eccentricities have excited, to become a minister of the Crown, if not Prime Minister himself; and all too on a basis of talent and achievement which if reduced to writing would be unworthy a penny-a-liner, and of debating power which if exercised at the 'Cogers'' would have emptied the room. I was forced to ask myself the question—Is it really possible that the mere stage and arena on which a man struts, can by its effects on the imaginations of men so transform his very complexion and personality in their eyes, as to entirely alter his outlook, standing, and fortune in this world? And for reply I was bound to answer,—not only possible, but certain. For it is demonstrable that if you can once make a man's name a household word by blowing on it sufficiently, and especially if it is in a cause like politics, where sides are taken, or in judicial evidence where there is room for discrepancies or differences of opinion, you will have gone a long way in rooting him in the imaginations or hearts of the people. The effect of mere publicity itself —of mere reverberation, of being isolated, brought out of the crowd, and set on high— by its effect on the imagination alone will do it. You have only to look at the way in which some poor Tichborne Claimant, some felon in the law courts, or pathetic disconsolate Jumbo, can by mere publicity so concentrate on himself public interest and attention, that for the hour he divides the sympathies of the nation with its rulers themselves, to feel what the effect of the same advertisement must be when the object of it cannot die with the day, or pass into oblivion by distance or lapse of time, but lives on under one's eyes, born anew every morning in the perennial flow of printed debate, each day bringing a new change of performance, a new occasion to men for the display of prejudice, partisanship, or pride. So clearly indeed did I perceive from the outset what the effect of this world-wide advertisement of his name and performance by the Press for the titillation of its readers' palates would be, that at a time when to have predicted his rise would have been to draw down on you the derision of all serious politicians, I ventured, in a work I was writing, to assert with confidence that he would rise, and that in no long time, to be a minister of the Crown; and when I found that a journal of the great power, candour, and seriousness of the *Spectator*, in order to neutralize the baneful effects of this world-wide advertisement, was obliged to have an editorial on him every few weeks, struggling to keep out the ocean with its broom (and with about as much hope of success as would attend the efforts of a regular physician to overtake the world-wide advertisement of some 'Holloway's pill'), I felt the more strongly that his success was assured.

Such was the part played in the rise of Lord Randolph Churchill by the mere echo and reverberation of his name in the Public Press, surrounding him, as it naturally did, in the mind of the multitude with an areola of real but vague and indefinite superiority. By its action on the imaginations of men alone, it dilated his essentially small bulk, as in a camera, until it became of world-wide importance, while at the same time it gilded, transmuted, and idealized it until it became the image and embodiment of power; it took him out of the ordinary mob of honourable members, and, like the birth of an heir-apparent in the direct line of legitimacy (for to the great masses of men the stamp of public reputation alone gives legitimacy), gave his party a name and object round which they could rally; and so indirectly gave him high claims on the reversion to the sovereignty. But if the Press by mere advertisement alone gave him in this way *general* bulk and prestige in the eyes of his party and the world, it was left for the operation of Party Politics to build for him a reputation for ability and character piecemeal and in *detail*; and that too, as I shall show further on, on a range and basis of ability and achievement smaller and meaner perhaps than in open competition has ever won high place in recorded history.

The Party journals, as I have said, although they would have blushed to have connected his name with the thought of Statesmanship *in general*, nevertheless, as was natural, snatched at any isolated remarks of his that could by any possibility lend a show of temperance and decency to his erratic speeches, and used these as weapons to beat their opponents withal; and as he opposed everything right and left that fell from the Government, hitting about him freely at all points of the compass, and, like a tipsy 'slogger,' was sure occasionally to get in an effective blow through the most experienced fence, these journals would pounce on it as a prize; and while passing lightly over the speech as a whole with the remark, perhaps, that it lacked form a little, or was disfigured in parts by personality or exaggeration, would turn their full emphasis on some isolated observation (generally a platitude I noticed), and characterize it as a very pointed example of acute and effective criticism. So pleased, indeed, were they to discover a lucid interval, or even the veriest commonplace that gave token of sanity in his long tirades of intemperance and exaggeration, that by that old trick of the mind, which like the old 'confidence' trick is ever green and young (the trick whereby courtiers will erect the one presentable feature of a prince into a general beauty, and fond and doting mothers the one generous action at the end of a long course of filial infamy into a reformation), they were so dazzled by the general imaginative halo with which the Press had surrounded him, that they saw in his veriest platitudes germs of a hidden statesmanship which, when age had brought discretion, and experience had damped the intemperance of youth, would yield a splendid fruition. And if perchance amid the flight of wide-winged shafts which passed for political criticism (most of which, however, either struck his own friends or the ceiling), one should happen to find its way anywhere near the target at which it was aimed, the Party journals would proceed to dig down into the dreary columns of debate to bring it up again to resurrection and life, would set it up on a pedestal and walk around it in admiration, surveying it on all sides, and unanimously proclaiming to all the world that here indeed was the making of a political reputation which the world would not soon or willingly let die.

Such was the transformation that, within the memory of all, his *intellectual* standing underwent in the eyes of Party-love, as one watched it during the short years of its inception and growth — a transformation, indeed, which may be seen going on at this hour. But not only his intellect, his very *character* also underwent a transformation under the same genial influence. So grateful indeed, as was natural, was his own party for the work of opposition and obstruction he was doing for them (however much they may have secretly disliked his means), that like the Irish, who condoned the murder of Carey, and transfigured his assassin into a kind of hero and martyr, they, to salve their consciences and justify to themselves their applause, gave to his most vulgar and insolent attacks all the gloss, phrase, and varnish of virtue. His most coarse and brutal thrusts they characterized by a fine euphemism as but a dash of devil-me-caredness—a breezy freshness of youth—which time would mollify; his sullen and most intemperate impudence and abuse were but a pretty insolence and sauciness; the rockets of abuse which he sent flying among friends and foes alike were but a healthy dislike of conventional formalisms; his want of reverence alike for age, ability, and experience was a natural aversion to a 'gang' of old fogies, or a genuine contempt for humbug.

In this way for party purposes (and themselves coming more and more under the illusion which by puffing they had produced) the Party journals gave a factitious and exaggerated importance to particular utterances of the noble lord, and so built up for him insidiously, and by piecemeal, a reputation for ability in *particular*, which for decency's sake they had not as yet the hardihood to affirm in *general* terms; while in the mean time the lower orders of Party journalism, by continuously writing up his tawdry metaphors, his caricatures, and his exaggerations (specimens of which we shall see further on), as the happiest efforts of genius, played on the imaginations of those inclined to his political views, and succeeded in getting these rhetorical efforts as seriously regarded as strokes of genius by the rank and file of the party, as the poetical efforts of Robert Montgomery were by their forefathers until Macaulay pricked the over-stuffed effigy and let out the sawdust.

Meanwhile, it was interesting to note the effect and reaction of all this on Lord Randolph Churchill himself. Swollen to the bursting point by the attention and interest which the Press had been the means of attracting to him, he be-rattled the stage worse than ever, delivering in the course of a short session some hundreds of obstructive and erratic speeches, and abusing in turn the time and dignity of the House by his successive appearances in one or other of his old and well-recognized characters. At one time he would run amuck of his own party, to its amusement, bewilderment, or dismay; at another, he would with mock-heroic indignation draw his little sword before the whole House, and pose as another Miltiades, the saviour of his country; while at another, he would be seen improving his reputation for diligence and industry by sitting over the details of measures, chattering and pecking at them like a daw, and calling it, as we have seen, 'fighting the measure clause by clause.'

More important, however, than the effects on Lord Randolph Churchill of the action of the Press and Party Politics, were their effects on the great body of the People themselves; and it is to this that I am now desirous of drawing the attention of the reader. What with the Press advertising him over the wide world as some new Barnum's wonder, and reporting his speeches verbatim, and in large type, not for their merits (as they themselves tacitly admitted), but to tickle the palates of that large class who in regard to serious politics are much like old Polonius, and must have 'a jig, or a tale of bawdry, or they sleep;' what with his obstructive tactics, which, good for immediate party ends, would if persisted in by minorities generally, render all government impossible; his brutal personalities which, although as congenial to the excited partizan as the secret daggers and poisoned chalices of the Borgias, would, if they became general, have honourable members at one another's throats within the week; what with a style of rhetoric and debate, which although, as I have said, if printed, would be worthy only of the poorest penny-a-liner, if spoken at the Cogers' Hall, would have emptied the room, was nevertheless regarded by speech-bound honourable members as so clever that the atrocity of characterizing Mr. Gladstone as 'the Moloch of Midlothian whose hands were literally dripping and reeking with blood,' was regarded by them as a bright particular stroke of genius which it were difficult to match;—what with all this, the effect was to fix him in the imagination of his party as a star of the first magnitude,—waverers who were still unconvinced by the reverberation of his name and the noise and uproar he was causing, being secretly converted, all their doubts and fears being allayed and smoothed away, by the hints and whispers that were dropped abroad that on him had fallen the mantle of the sainted Beaconsfield himself. In this way this steady and unbroken course of insolence, buffoonery, and abuse, in a man who had now reached his thirty-fifth year, was by a kind of alchemy of the imagination gradually transfigured into a radiant and golden career of youth, pluck, and political promise ; the illusion being either engendered directly by puffing, or passed like an infection from one class to another down the descending links in the chain of society (outside the circle of the really cultured), from nobleman and 'gentleman' to the Music Hall *habitué* and the Conservative working man.

His earliest supporters were drawn from the ranks of his own party in the House itself. The fine old-crusted Tories, the country gentlemen who sat in mass behind their leaders on the Front Bench, and who were humourously described by one genial and impartial observer as so afflicted with ennui, indolence, and speechlessness, that as the clock turned to the dinner hour, they trooped away to one diversion, to return when Lord Randolph rose to another—these gentlemen, who regarded him as diverting and amusing, but of no political significance, were so secretly delighted by his brutal attacks on one whom they held as their mortal foe, that whenever he rose to speak they applauded him to the echo, and were thus the first who by their countenance and encouragement warmed to their bosoms the asp that was to sting them. For I will, without hesitation, give them this as their dowry, that whatever Lord Randolph Churchill may do for them and their class in the future, he has already, by the support and impetus he has given to essentially Radical opinion, let down the peg of old Tory policy to so low a pitch, that whatever party may in future happen to be in power is pledged already to carry out reforms which must be fatal in the end to that landed and aristocratic predominance they so much prize — reforms which but for him might by a united Tory party have been honourably postponed for many a year to come. By their unreflecting haste to applaud the dishonourable tactics practised by him on their opponents, they gave edge and efficiency to the very weapon which was to do execution on themselves; for with Lord Randolph Churchill as their leader to flirt with triumphant Democracy, one may justly parody the language of Shakspeare and say, that "not poppy, nor mandragora, nor all the drowsy syrups of the world shall ever medicine them again to that sweet old Tory sleep which they owed yesterday."

Descending in lineal sequence from the Squires, his next recruits were drawn from the large body of Villa Residents living in the centres or suburbs of great cities and towns, men as a rule engaged in commerce or manufactures, whose conversation and point of view are to a large extent the echo of the *Times* newspaper, and who, from their alleged absence of general culture, are known among men of culture as the 'Philistines.' These men originally and instinctively liked neither the smell nor composition of the hotch-potch and patent-treacle which Lord Randolph Churchill was offering them under the name of Tory Democracy, but being ever alive to the lightest note or whisper that may chance to drop over the outside walls from the higher spheres of 'society,' and being reassured by the plaudits of the Squires within; being secretly delighted too with any personal attack, however coarse, that gave voice and echo to their deep dislike of the Liberal leader, they were not long in enrolling themselves among his admirers, and after a little incubation among his followers. Besides, from their imperfect culture they really thought his style and rhetoric brilliant, and himself a miracle of cleverness. I have heard them as they came into the city in the morning by train exclaiming to one another over the top of their newspapers: "Splendid fellow, Churchill. Brilliant speech last night. Didn't he let into that old humbug. He's the coming man no doubt." And on glancing down my own paper to see where the brilliancy specially appeared, I would come to the passage that most probably gave rise to the exclamation (all the rest of the speech being mere commonplace) in the remark perhaps that Mr. Gladstone was 'a purblind and sanctimonious Pharisee,' or John Bright a 'senile and infatuated hypocrite!' Such was the style of political metaphor and criticism which these men really regarded as evidence of ability so great that (when delivered on the floor of the great House of Commons, and not merely scribbled in a penny paper by some 'low fellow' possibly out at elbows) it was sufficient to mark him out as the coming man; although in the body of these same speeches were sentiments so radical and even socialistic in tendency, as to have helped to bring the destructive policy of which they were the symptoms (and which these men most dreaded) within measurable distance of practical legislation. But with the glare of notoriety full upon him, and reassured, as

I have said, by the plaudits of the Squires, these residents of the villas passed lightly over the obnoxious sentiments, and gave diligent ear only to the more attractive and exciting personalities. And here, again, one may truly say that Democracy being now here, and determined by open or secret courses to have a larger share than heretofore in the earth's produce, and as there are only two heritages out of which rightly or wrongly it can be carved,—the land, and the commercial and manufacturing capital of the country,—that these gentlemen should dream that so lively and unscrupulous a circus-rider as Lord Randolph Churchill, whom a healthy instinct should have taught them to shun as the Devil from the beginning, will fail to settle on one or the other of these, or both, according as the shouts of the victorious and applauding multitude shall dictate—"Cæsar, thou hast subdued their judgments also."

The next order of recruits whom Lord Randolph Churchill succeeded in gaining to his allegiance, through the action of the Press and of Party Politics, was drawn from the large army of Clerks, Travellers, and Dependants generally of the two former classes. Fortified by the applause and good opinion of the higher members of the party, they found no difficulty in regarding him from the outset as the 'coming man.' Unlike their masters, however, they took him from the first seriously, and not as a joke, and that too without hesitation, repulsion, or fear. Without property themselves, or the sense of responsibility which it brings; with little or no hope of rising out of the positions in which they serve, and desirous above all things of maintaining that tone and appearance of 'respectability' which alone on their small means can distinguish them from the rude unwashed throng; debarred too by their position and training of the opportunities of any real or genuine culture; with no sense of historical perspective; and nothing to break the clouds of illusion in which they are enveloped; they regarded this erratic knight-errant in the cause of Tory Democracy as a kind of hero from the very outset, and supported him with a more fiery zeal than their masters themselves.

With that mortal reverence and awe with which men of this type regard any one in the 'position' of a Cabinet Minister, the very idea that Lord Randolph Churchill should take the field against all comers, and like another Jack the Giant-Killer, should not only dare to beard the Prime Minister himself, but should flaunt his own leaders as a 'gang of old fogies' much too 'slow' to lead a great historic party, so overawed and stunned their imaginations as to irradiate and transfigure his long trail of insolence and abuse into a glorious career of political audacity and pluck; and with the Press blowing on him as with a bellows from behind, and more than all with the whispers that came to them that he was the legitimate heir to the Beaconsfield tradition;—all compelled the conviction that here indeed must be a man of unique and extraordinary genius. But the greatest satire of all was, that at the very time when respectable Party journals were for decency's sake obliged to apologize for his outrages on the grounds of youth, hot-headedness, and inexperience, these gentlemen would boldly avow their honest admiration for these very outrages (his insolence, I noticed, they always spoke of as 'pluck,' and his newspaper style of vituperation as 'extraordinary power of language'); and among their own circle of friends you would overhear such outbursts of enthusiasm on his behalf as these: "Wonderful fellow,

Churchill! awfully clever, and with any amount of pluck! Sir Stafford a good sound man, but too slow, you know! Churchill is the man we want," until one was obliged to stop one's ears and run for it.

The last order of adherent whom Lord Randolph Churchill succeeded in gaining to his standard was the Conservative Working-man, for whose character indeed, if not judgment, all must feel the highest respect. Like his more ambitious brother—the City Clerk—it was both natural and right that (with that weight of habit and tradition on him which with most men is the best guarantee of sobriety and respectability) he too should feel more confidence in adhering to the ancient ways, and acquiescing in the ancient structure of society in Church and State, than in any new-fangled schemes for the reconstruction of society, which however necessary, and in the end inevitable, were as yet raw and untried. Warmed as he was by the feeling that his opinions were in accordance with those of his masters (and in this the Conservative Working-man is most loyal), and having besides his own proper pride and sense of dignity, it was natural that when he found a person sufficiently accredited coming forward and announcing that he was the representative of Tory Democracy, he should feel that his own importance in the State would no longer be ignored, and that he would be more respected than under the older Tory *régimes;* and in consequence might go bravely forward, nothing doubting, prepared to fall down in admiration and worship as at the feet of a new and lawful king.

Now as these two latter classes—the Clerks and the Conservative Working-men—made up numerically his most numerous *clientèle,* and having the votes were in consequence the most important; and as they were just at that intellectual point of view where his clap-trap rhetoric and metaphor seemed to them, like a music-hall song, to be the very high-water mark of genius itself; it became at once a foregone conclusion that having secured these he had now nothing more to do but to go on boldly and to conquer.

In this way, then, Lord Randolph Churchill gradually succeeded in fixing his authority on the neck of his party, and in gathering around him a compact and enthusiastic body of adherents—primarily by the puffing of the Press (for all mere advertisement, if on an extensive scale, by taking a man out of his surroundings gives him greater bulk and radiance in the common eye, and so by its mere action on the imagination becomes an indirect species of puffing); secondly, by the action of Party Politics, which, too, by a kind of mental alchemy converts even the grosser and baser elements into lustres; thirdly, by his style and quality of rhetoric and debate, which although they bore as much resemblance to real oratory and statesmanship as the style and quality of a penny-a-liner do to Shakspeare, nevertheless by the great masses were quite as highly appreciated; and lastly, by his character and procedure generally, which (in connection with his so-called youth, and owing to the high stage on which he acted, and the antagonists with whom he was brought into contact), although vulgar, insolent, and abusive to a degree almost beyond belief, nevertheless were regarded by the pit and gallery as entirely heroic, transmuted as they were by party-love into a splendid audacity and virtue. The result of all this was so to burn his name and personality into the popular imagination, that when the smaller but more reputable portion of his party resolved at last to shake him off, their voices were drowned by such a chorus of opposition from the pit and gallery, that they were obliged in despair to relinquish the attempt. His influence, meanwhile, was, as one could have foreseen, gradually becoming more and more assured, till you now saw it openly making itself recognized. One compliment after another was paid to him by various portions of his party in town and country. He was made chairman of the National Union of Conservative Associations, President of the Primrose League, and altogether soon became universally regarded by the rank and file of the party out of doors as one of its most prominent, able, and rising members.

And now, it may be asked, what was the attitude of the Press in regard to this transformation in Public Opinion?

Having for its own ends, and the delectation of its readers at the breakfast-table, been the means of giving him notoriety, and this notoriety (by its action on the imagination) having united with certain factitious elements to produce a glorified image of genius and character altogether irrecognizable in the original portrait, the Press now began, like another Pygmalion or barbarian idolator, to worship the idealized image or overgrown simulacrum of a deity which its own hands had created; bending before it in admiration and worship at all points, and that too although in the mean time neither his style, manner, or form of achievement had, as itself admitted, in any way changed. Having begun by giving their readers a crude and literal image of him as he was, which these in their turn idealized, transmuted, and gilded by the action of their minds (for no mere brazen serpent once erected on high, and on which all men have looked, is ever again the same brazen image as it was before), they ended by accepting from their readers this glorified and transmuted image as his true likeness. The respective organs of opinion, with that dignified complacency which is so essential to their influence, began gradually, you observed (in proportion as their constituents out of doors were being impressed by his achievements), to take him more seriously. They spoke vaguely, but often, of his cleverness, his sarcasm, his brilliancy, his power of argument and debate, his pluck, his audacity, and the like; and would search, if they had to go to the very centre, till they had recovered the needle of commonplace out of a whole haystack of absurdity; the Comic Papers alone as chartered libertines still continuing, however, to picture him as before, but with some mitigation perhaps of severity. Even the *Spectator*, which had struggled breathlessly, as we saw, in its endeavour to keep out the inundation with its broom, now strove hard, with its usual fairness and candour, to find a single spot of sound and solid substance (even under the microscope) on which to plant a fixed and steady compliment, but in vain.

Meanwhile the effect of all this was to stimulate Lord Randolph Churchill to still greater exertions, and to confirm and strengthen his own belief in the efficacy, for his own objects, of the style and tactics he had been pursuing. Indeed at this period (speaking roughly about four years after his first appearance) he outdid all his previous record in prodigality of abuse, exaggeration, and personality, tearing a passion to very tatters to split the ears of the groundlings (who had the votes), defying his opponents, flouting his own leaders, and heaping on them in the face of the world every form and variety of contumely; while at the same time he increased his reputation for serious work and industry, by sitting watching more closely than ever the rat-holes and details of the measures and policy that passed before him. But it was soon felt that this fussy, impotent, and fretful show of activity would not atone for the wild and incalculable flights of policy to which he was subject. So extraordinary indeed did his political procedure at last become; so inconsistent were his doctrines with those of the party to which he professed to belong; so loose, crude, and dangerous did his opinions seem to them to be (his opinions on landed property, on county government, his sympathy real or pretended with the Irish patriots, and the like); so light and facile was his power of executing a *volte face* on all possible subjects according to the political exigencies of the moment or the direction of the popular gale; such was his want of tact, his bad taste, and his growing reputation for unscrupulousness, that he succeeded at last in thoroughly alienating the recognized leaders of his own party, and in spreading a general dismay through all its ranks.

The Tory squires who had been the first to applaud his coarse and brutal attacks on the Liberal Leader (and who indeed to this day can listen to this abuse with pleasure and applause), were the first to take the alarm—which soon, however, became general among honourable members, who, being on the spot, saw most clearly the dangers to which, from division, the party was now exposed. They paused for a moment in their encouragement, silenced their applause, and threatened to desert him in mass. The *Standard*, as the leading organ of the party, feeling already that he was doomed, stepped at once to the front, and giving voice to what (had it not been for the exigencies of Party or the breakfast-table) had long been the real opinion of all sound and thoughtful politicians in and out of Parliament, told him in other words that he was an impudent, un-blushing, impostor, with no more real knowledge of politics than an overgrown schoolboy, and too ignorant even to know the depths of his own ignorance; and that, in a word, he had better take himself off and be gone. And had the result indeed depended on these honourable members and their organ in the Press, there can be little doubt that he would forthwith have been thrown incontinently overboard. But they had reckoned without their host. It was not for nothing that the united bellows of the Press (that of the *Standard* included) had been blowing on his name and reputation during all these years, until, like some Holloway's Pill, it stared on you from every placard and boarding—in newspapers, magazines, railway stations, and books. So deeply indeed had they burnt his name into the imaginations of men throughout the length and breadth of the land, that like the wise general he was, when attacked he had only to do nothing, and for reply to snap his fingers, whistle, and go on his own way. For it is a demonstrable truth (the bearing of which on democratic governments we shall see farther on), that if you snatch the first man you meet in the street, and give him for a term of years the political advertisement that was given to Lord Randolph Churchill (whether avowedly for the interest and amusement of readers or no, matters not), you shall, by its mere effect on the imaginations of men, put him on so lofty a pedestal, that no mere political inconsistencies, no atrocities of speech or political audacities, no mere clique of editors and honourable members, nothing indeed (except perhaps a personal felony) shall take him down again. And if one thing more than another could prove, and that conclusively, that his rise was due to puffing, and puffing alone (in the sense in which I have described it), it is the fact that the *Standard*, the daily organ of the Conservative Party, after watching his career for four or five years and secretly conniving for party purposes at his unscrupulous tactics, and moreover at his rising reputation, should have been able to discover so little real substance in him, that when at last it was obliged to speak out, it had to confess that he was nothing more or less than an impudent political fraud, with no more knowledge than an overgrown school-boy—and that too, if I mistake not, within a very few weeks of the time of his accession to the Cabinet, if indeed not after. But be this as it may, Lord Randolph Churchill when they attempted to remove him could safely snap his fingers at them, and go gaily on his way; for however easy it may be for a clique of journalists and politicians to put a man on the throne, once there—and with all the power of the State, that is to say public opinion, at his back—it is not so easy to take him down again. And as result, we found that when about the time of this *émeute* a junction of the Parnellites with the Conservatives enabled the latter to defeat the Liberal Government and come into power, Lord Randolph Churchill, by the hold he had acquired on his party out of doors, was able to dictate his own terms in the formation of the new Government, of which he became one of the most prominent members, and at last,* as we now see, leader of the House of Commons.

Such in brief was the rise of Lord Randolph Churchill as it went on from day to day under the eyes and in the memory of all—a rise unirradiated by real greatness at any point in its course, and accomplished by such a combination of cheap expedients (as I shall now show) before the eyes of what is called the free and enlightened English people as has nowhere been known within living memory, and well deserves therefore to live in history—a career unbrightened from first to last by any gleam of generosity, nobility, elevation of political principle, or honourable political practice; and worse than all, as I shall now endeavour to make good, unirradiated by any but the cheapest, meanest, and lowest order of ability—an order of ability, however,

* Autumn '86.

which I grant you is so level with all that is superficial and ignorant in human nature, that if well planted, so as to command the great masses of men, it will like a debauching harlotry succeed where virtue fails, and outface the modesty of genius itself. A combination of cheap expedients, I say, which I foresaw from the first would be successful, and which moreover, unless burnt into the public mind with the same persistency as his own name has been, can be played over and over again with equal certainty of success. If, as Burke says, the road to great place should not be made too easy, it may well be said of Lord Randolph Churchill, that instead of forcing his way up the rugged steeps to the summit by sheer power (as was the case with Burke himself), he has been blown thither like thistle-down by puffing and levity only. No Æsop's fly sitting on the axle of a chariot-wheel, and imagining itself the cause of all the dust that rose, could be more ridiculous than Lord Randolph Churchill sitting on the wheel of the parliamentary chariot, as it was driven around the world by the Press, and imagining that all the commotion caused was due to his sole power and ability. To do what in me lies to prevent the really disgraceful exhibition of another rise to power by the same arts, I propose now to examine Lord Randolph Churchill's actual achievements in detail,—what he has done or said; what the scope of his political principles is; what range and quality of ability are involved in his style, tactics, and principles; what the tricks are by which he has imposed on his admirers; and the like,—and for this end I propose to make use of the volume of his public speeches prepared and edited by one of his earliest admirers—speeches which, with all that was unworthy in his purely parliamentary procedure eliminated, present him in his most sober, respectable, and serious garb.

Before doing this, however, it were as well perhaps to endeavour to fix his place as a mere Orator or Public Speaker, in order the better to eliminate at the outset from the factors that have gone to make up his success the acknowledged effects of popular oratory on the great masses of men.

CHAPTER V.

LORD RANDOLPH CHURCHILL AS ORATOR.

In the present chapter I propose to consider Lord Randolph Churchill with reference rather to the style, manner, and other external qualities of his speeches than to the depth, range, and variety of their subject matter (which I have left for my next chapter)—to consider him, that is to say, with reference rather to his qualities as an Orator than as a Statesman.

On the few occasions on which I had the opportunity of hearing him speak in the House of Commons, his remarks were more or less short and fragmentary in character, being either, as I have said, of the nature of interruption, or of captious and impertinent comment and objection, raised apparently for obstructive purposes, and bearing about as much relation to serious debate as the wanton and obtrusive comments of schoolboys do to the serious conversation of their parents or elders. This apparent absence of seriousness and sincerity was seen, I may perhaps explain, rather in the import and matter of his remarks, than in their style or manner, which from my old experience of public speakers, and on the principle of *ex pede Herculem*, I felt was not the style or manner of either a rapid, brilliant, or effective speaker. His voice was deep, harsh, and without inflexion, and although there was little or no halting and stammering, there was just that degree of slowness and hesitation in his utterance which made me feel that his natural powers in the way of free and spontaneous speech must be strictly limited and confined. Being aware, however, of the great difference sometimes observed between a man's oratorical powers when making a few discursive, negative, or critical remarks, and these same powers when fully engaged on some large constructive and connected speech, and feeling that it would not be fair to make the one the measure of the other; being desirous also of dealing only with such large characteristics of his style as from their inherent and essential nature could, when eliminated and defined, be fairly expected to hold good of his oratory at any time or in any place, I had determined (should no further opportunity present itself of hearing him in a connected speech) to deal with the *matter* only of his collected speeches, as on these speeches all claims that could be put forward in his behalf as a serious statesman up to the time of his advent into the Cabinet must be founded. But knowing as I did the effect of mere oratory as such on men's estimation of a man's powers, and the great part it plays in the politics of the present time, I still longed for an opportunity of hearing him in some well-pondered and connected speech, as this would enable me to give to my sketch of his political career a greater fulness and completeness. By good fortune my desire was at last gratified, and an opportunity presented itself of hearing him in the speech of two hours' duration which he delivered to his constituents at Paddington on the eve of the last election.

A friend of mine, a man of untrammelled eye, not to be daunted or overawed by mere reputation or prestige, and entirely without personal or political bias, offered to accompany me to the place of meeting; and as we walked along speculating on what we were likely to hear, we agreed that if he should really turn out to be a brilliant, fluent, and effective speaker, that fact alone would in some measure help to explain, if not to justify, his sudden rise and popularity. On arriving at the Riding School in which the meeting was to be held, we found it packed and thronged by an immense assembly of his supporters and admirers; and as admission was by ticket, and all rude or hostile elements were in consequence excluded, all the conditions essential to a free and effective speech were abundantly present. The subject of his remarks, too, which was to be the great Home Rule problem then agitating the country and exercising all minds, although it had already been severely thrashed out by the Press and by the leading men of all political parties, still left abundant room for original handling, constructive ingenuity, and all the arts and graces of the rhetorician and orator. After some delay Lord Randolph Churchill at last entered the hall amid the waving and cheering of the dense audience, and as he made his way forward to the platform in evening dress, and with a large red rose in his button-hole, he seemed to be a slim, narrow-shouldered man of about or below the medium height, his movements having more or less of that slow and *blazé*-aristocratic air which one would have expected rather in the lounger of a West End Club than in an active and pushing politician. His face was small and pale, his head high and conical, and his features were readily distinguishable as those which during the last few years have been made so familiar to us by means of prints, photographs, and cartoons. There were the same large and prominent eyes; the deep heavy moustache with its twisted ends; the prominent ears; the short, aggressive nose; the expression neutral or complacent, and with just a shade of sullenness in it about the cheek and eye; while over the whole face there was (what is not seen in the photographs) a milk-white paleness, which, taken with the large prominence of the eye, gave the appearance, from the distance where I was sitting, of physical delicacy, almost of sybaritic effeminacy.

When the shouting and cheering which greeted his entrance had subsided, and all was again quiet, he rose and began to speak in the slow and deliberate manner which you would have expected from his *blazé*-aristocratic air, but in a voice which at once struck you by its deep, almost harsh tones, and which, although corresponding in a measure to the sullen expression of the face and eye, arrested attention by its marked contrast with his appearance of physical weakness and effeminacy.

A few introductory remarks delivered in these slow, deep, and somewhat harsh tones, thanking the electors for the honour they had done him in again choosing him as their representative, passed off without comment or remark, and brought him at once face to face with his celebrated 'Paddington Address,' which had then just recently been published, and which had caused such a feeling of indignation throughout the country, from its tone of cold, calculated, and heartless scurrility. The remarks he had to make on this matter were delivered in the same slow, monotonous manner with which he began; each sentence ending in a fall of the voice, followed by just sufficient pause to enable him to see to the end of the next sentence without stammering or stumbling by the way. The audience, as is so often the case when a vast throng of men come together to do honour to one whom they regard with admiration, seemed to be in a state of nervous titillation and excitement; and at the first reference to this episode of the 'Address,' seemed to anticipate some brilliant and wonderful exhibition of rhetoric, sarcasm, or wit. Nothing of this nature came, however, nothing but the harsh and grinding cadence and uniformity of the sentences, cold and passionless and slow. And when the end and upshot of it all was to reiterate that he had carefully weighed the words of his 'address,' and that they were all true, the great audience, like some demoralized mob that had lost its head, cheered the base and unworthy sentiment until the rafters rang with the applause. The truth was, that instead of a number of separate and isolated individuals exercising separate and independent judgment, they had already run together into a herd, and were in that state of mental tiptoe and expectancy that makes men ready to applaud atrocities of speech or conduct which in their individual and better judgments they would have reprobated. Passing on from this ugly episode, he next by a kind of *tuquoque*, and by way of indirect justification of himself, attempted to fasten on Mr. Gladstone the same charge of personal scurrility that had been brought against himself. Mr.

Gladstone had, it appears, in reply to some question addressed to him in reference to Mr. Peter Rylands (who had deserted him in his Home Rule policy), made use of the expression that 'our old friend Peter has gone to the bad.' On this palpably facetious and, I presume, merely passing remark Lord Randolph Churchill seized as a godsend, and it was evident from the manner in which he set out that he was determined to make the most of it. With a show of seriousness and solemnity over this veriest of trifles which was in itself a study, he asked the audience in his slow and heavy way what they could think of a statesman who could so indulge in personal abuse as to publicly assert that 'our old friend Peter had gone to the bad.' Not content with putting it thus plainly, he continued to turn it over on all sides, placing it in different lights, revolving and tumbling round it until you could have gone to sleep, and finally ended like some heavy quadruped of the field, by rolling over it. My friend, who had waited patiently and given him ample time to kindle the fire of oratory and passion, finding that, instead of the flames of eloquence leaping forth, nothing issued but this slow and wooden monotony, without humour, wit, or passion, at last ventured to break the silence, and whispered secretly into my ear the ominous words—a bore! The audience, too, feeling instinctively the note of insincerity that ran through this feeble attempt to extract a subject of vituperation out of so palpable a trifle, and with a finer sense of measure and proportion than their master, evidently began to feel wearied, and certain of their number gave symptoms of impatience for work of a more red-handed character. So deeply indeed had the idea of the lively lampooner got associated in their minds with his name, that like boys who pull a monkey's tail to get it to perform its favourite tricks, they commenced to throw out trails across his path; and whenever he mentioned any name that was likely to form a subject of abuse, they hooted and cheered in order to draw him on, but in vain,—he continued on his slow and stolid course unheeding. But although he was not to be drawn out of the course he had marked out for himself, he nevertheless had no intention of falling below his own reputation, or of disappointing the expectations of his hearers, but had come down prepared with deep-dyed patches of more express and concentrated abuse, which he plastered on here and there at intervals along the course of his speech. To become lively, however, was too much for him. He had already been speaking some twenty minutes or more, and, for my own part, all hope of finding in him the lively buffoon of public opinion had long been resigned. It was evidently a false reputation (this of his being a lively speaker), engendered by the Press, which in intending to characterize the lively *matter* of his speeches, used words and phrases which covered their *manner* also; and thus the public had read into his printed speeches precisely that amount of rapidity and life which they had been taught to associate with his name. Nothing could be further from the fact than to imagine him a rapid or a lively speaker. On the contrary, a more heavy, sullen, and dreary speaker, for one making any pretence to the art, I have rarely or never heard; and when he produced his first red-dyed patch of personal abuse by calling Mr. Gladstone a madman, and went on to advise him (plagiarizing from Lord Beaconsfield) to sail for Anticyra, there to take hellebore as a cure for it, the whole affair was so leaden, dull, and long drawn-out, that you saw his point long before he got to it, and as a piece of wit it fell in consequence dead as lead.

He had already been speaking for half an hour or more, and his remarks had hitherto been directed rather to interest and attract the gallery, than the graver portions of his audience. He now came to the more serious aspects of his speech; but lest his audience should be lying in wait for a joke when his intention was to be quite serious, he began by explaining that he was about to enter on a long and connected argument against Home Rule, which would demand all their consideration, and to which he invited their most close and earnest attention.

All being again quiet, he made preparations for his new departure, glanced at his notes, and walked slowly up and down (his hands in his waistcoat) with all the pose and solemnity of an aged statesman. It was curious to note the impression this pose of the serious political teacher, coming as it did from a politician of yesterday, with such history and antecedents, made on a large portion of the audience, and the difficulty they found in making it harmonize with his traditionary reputation. For no sooner had he opened his argument by the grave announcement that Ireland was an island, than the audience, who were still on the flighty tip-toe of titillation and expectancy, burst into laughter, as if the statement were but the preliminary to some concealed joke of more than usual brilliancy. He stopped, assured them that he was really in earnest, and that on this apparent platitude of Ireland being an island hung an argument of great force and cogency. Having in this way quelled their levity, he was again allowed to proceed, and at once plunged into a long dissertation through which ran indeed a thin strand of argument, but of so light and unimpressive a nature that little more remains of it with me now than the upshot, which was to this effect— that as the Catholic Parliament of Tyrconnel had persecuted the Protestants, and the Protestant Parliament of Grattan had persecuted the Catholics, and in both instances the strong hand of England had had to intervene to keep the peace and see that justice was done, the result would be the same again to-morrow if Ireland were allowed Home Rule. Now, as an argument this was of course all right enough, and would have answered its purpose sufficiently well; but so long drawn-out was it, so tedious in its development, that the audience, before it was done, were palpably wearied and exhausted, and you saw them here and there secretly yawning behind their handkerchiefs or hats. The truth is, one had heard so much of his rhetorical brilliancy, his lightness and audacity, that one pictured him as some rapid and brilliant *sabreur* with his keen and swift thrust and defence, as some brilliant, bright, glib-tongued, and caustic wit and humourist; and to this impression indeed his very impertinences, buffooneries, and antics lent support rather than otherwise. But no impression could have had less real foundation. No elephant jumping over bars and tables in emulation of a light-heeled monkey could have been more dull, ponderous, and leaden-footed. His argument, as I have said, was drawn out to an interminable length, dragging its slow length along with such pause and interval between the sentences that they must have been jewels of wit or wisdom to have borne the strain; and had the audience been hostile, the opportunities offered for interruption and obstruction would have speedily brought it to a standstill. The yawning in consequence continued, and even spread as he went along, those who still held out being kept awake either by their interest in the subject itself, or by their anticipation of some joke or piece of sarcasm, which however only came at rare and uncertain intervals. He himself seemed to be not altogether at home in this element of serious discourse, but walked cautiously along it like a man on a plank, and with so little momentum that the slightest disturbance was sufficient to shake his balance, and throw him off the track; one poor devil who was standing against the door, and who in the heat of the room every now and again drew the bolt to let in a breath of fresh air, distracting completely the attention of the room (a thing that would be impossible under the spell of a great orator), and so seriously disturbing his balance that at last he came to a standstill altogether. Some of the audience, who still hoped to get him on to his more accustomed element of personality, continued to draw herring-trails across his path as he went along, but without success. He trudged onward as if carrying a load of most momentous import on a precarious and uncertain footing, every now and then lighting up the way with a red-glaring patch of vituperation, and struggling to throw a show of force and conviction into his remarks by stertorously beating the fist of one hand on to the palm of the other— much in the manner in which you have seen some belated minister beat the pulpit when his argument was weak, or his fertility of thought and invention were beginning to fail.

When you read his speech in the morning's newspapers, the long trail of words of which it was made up seemed spontaneous enough (for, as I have said, you can always read *into* a printed speech just that amount of rapidity and animation which you have been accustomed to associate with the character and style of the speaker); but when you heard it delivered, it was slow, painfully constrained, and instead of being emitted with lightness, fluency, and above all rapidity, was tediously protracted; so that with his deep harsh voice and want of inflexion, the speech as a whole went grating along like the rasping of a keel over a gravelly bottom.

Of the *matter of* his collected speeches I shall have more to say in my next chapter, but of this particular speech, which occupied about two hours in the delivery, I may remark here, that there was little or no meat or nourishment in it, that it was little more than an elongated skeleton of words, with a thin skin of argument stretched over them to keep them together. No thought, I can safely say, above the veriest commonplace of the newspapers, lifted its head anywhere over the dreary waste to arrest your attention; no thought, political, social, or moral, that gave the least indication of grasp, penetration, or power. The allusions too and metaphors with which his speech was stuck round were of the most common and tawdry character, and so painfully wire-drawn and elongated were they, that you could anticipate them and go to sleep. Besides, in his remarks on men and things, there was no measure or gradation; his characterizations were altogether out of proportion to their object; all was strained, in extremes, and in the superlative degree. If a thing was bad, it was characterized as 'atrocious,' or 'abominable,' or 'unparalleled in its infamy'; if a man's conduct was bad, it was 'monstrous,' 'idiotic,' 'bloodthirsty,' 'unscrupulous,' or of like import; while to supply the place of a free and spontaneous utterance, he had recourse to the repetition of whole phrases, or parts of sentences, in the manner so familiar to me in the 'third-rate

Coger.' Instead, for example, of saying that 'a nation can never be prosperous, happy, or free until,' &c., he would say, 'a nation can never be prosperous, a nation can never be happy, a nation can never be free until,' &c., accompanying each phrase or clause of the sentence with a bend of the body forwards, and an emphatic gesture of the hand, in the manner which the reader will no doubt have often noticed in the tedious and would-be impressive stump-orator.

My friend, who had long resigned himself to the boredom of the speech, could at last bear it no longer, and at some pause or turn of the discourse whispered to me, "If Lord Randolph Churchill is what they call a lively speaker, what must the 'old gang' have been?" He had already gone on for nearly an hour and a half, and the audience indeed, many of them, seemed to be feeling much like my friend; they had seen their hero, and having given up all hopes of his falling a-cursing any farther for the night, considered the show as good as at an end; those in the back part of the room, who could get out without too much difficulty, dribbling away quietly and imperceptibly along the side walls to the door. Wearied out ourselves at last by the prolonged dulness and monotony, we also made our way to the door, the last words we heard as we passed into the open evening being his accusation (in the old slow, harsh, and monotonous style) of the Irish members in the House of Commons being kept by 'Yankee gold.' Slow, slow, heavy as lead, was our verdict as we got outside. Had the speech, by greater rapidity and animation in delivery, been compressed into half an hour (I myself read it next day in full in the *Times* in less than twenty minutes), it would have been tolerable enough; but stretched as it was on a hot summer's night over two mortal hours—unless a man were maddened with party-rage, or so drunk with admiration in the presence of his god as to convert all his platitudes into oracles of gold as they fell, it was indeed difficult to be borne.

Such in a general way were the leading characteristics of this speech of Lord Randolph Churchill's, as, without personal or party bias, they impressed themselves on my mind at the time—characteristics so typical of his style and manner, and so inherent in their very nature, that they must hold good of his speeches at any time or in any place. Altogether a most slow, poor, and ineffectual speech, harsh and monotonous, such as one could hear any day in the pulpit or market-place—a speech that can only be described by negatives, the matter being of so poor and second-rate a quality that had it been printed in a magazine to be judged by experts (instead of being delivered to an indiscriminating crowd by a Cabinet Minister) it would have been passed over unheeded; the manner and style cold, pinched, and passionless to a degree, without lightness, facility, fluency, or grace. Instead of his allusions and metaphors falling in easy and dazzling profusion along his track, as is the manner of great orators, the few that did appear were so long drawn-out (as in his 'naviget Anticyram') as to fall flat and dead. There was no spontaneous fire in the speech, as one would have imagined from his reputation; on the contrary, the whole seemed to be a prepared and closet performance, cold and heartless in its calculated ingenuity of abuse, without lightness, vivacity, or grace; the only appearance of animation being, as I have said, the effort to give to his exaggerations and platitudes the air and similitude of seriousness and truth by forcibly beating them out with one hand on the palm of the other. No single quality of the orator (and I watched carefully) anywhere appeared—neither rapidity, spontaneity, fluency, passion, earnestness, or heat. Had his personalities been thrown off rapidly and with spirit, although caricatures, and often brutal in their coarseness, they would (so great a point in oratory is rapidity) have answered their purpose for the moment, and been effective enough; but when prepared in cold blood, and tediously drawn out in a speech of two hours' duration, they became wearisome. Slow, slow, was the word that best expressed it all; with nothing to redeem it from boredom itself but the titillation and expectancy kept up by his name and reputation, the excitement of party warfare, and the absorbing interest at the moment of the great Home Rule question on which he was engaged. Had he gone with his speech to the Cogers' Hall, with no reputation at his back to excite expectation and turn his poor and tawdry personalities into gold, he would, I can confidently testify, have been listened to from the outset with ennui, and if he had continued would have gradually emptied the room. It is simply incredible that he could have ever established a reputation for oratory in the open arena and competition of the world; and only proves again to me what can be done by a man of the most limited oratorical power in the House of Commons, where he is seen of all the world, and where the Press blows his every word into every eye,—in the House of Commons, composed as it chiefly is of members who, from their antecedents and habits of life, make no pretence to oratory as such, and have had little or no scope for its exercise.

I am of course only too well aware how overdrawn my description of Lord Randolph Churchill's oratory will seem to those who have not yet got their eye on the power of political puffing to gild a man's natural powers, and transform mediocrity into genius; and it is precisely because I desire to bring this matter to the test, and not from any the least personal or political bias, that I have selected a concrete example in the person of the noble lord, and have endeavoured to emphasize only such leading and larger features of his style and manner as from their essential, inherent, and central character will be found when brought to the test to hold true of his oratory at any time or under any conditions. And when I think of the esteem in which oratory is held at the present day, and of the important part it plays or is believed to play in our political system, and then consider that by its supposed possession a man who is not even a 'third-rate Coger' has been enabled to climb to the uppermost offices of State, I am simply struck dumb with amazement at the thought of what puffing and a raised platform will do for men in this world. And when, furthermore, I think of the range of qualities, intellectual and moral, which have called forth this world-wide advertisement, I cannot too strongly repeat my conviction that whatever the *future* of Lord Randolph Churchill may be, the methods by which he *rose* to power have been a greater blow to all those ideals which men hold dear than any which have been employed in my time.

In the next chapter I shall direct attention to the *matter* of his public speeches, with the object of discovering whether his claim to the title of Statesman has any more real foundation in fact than his claim to the title of Orator.

CHAPTER VI.

LORD RANDOLPH CHURCHILL AS STATESMAN.

In examining the political speeches of Lord Randolph Churchill with the view of determining the special characteristics of the *matter* of which they are composed, as distinct from their *style and manner*, and of discovering, if possible, the depth and range of ability on which a success so swift and unprecedented as his has been built, I propose to consider, as I have said, only his most deliberate and well-grounded utterances as contained in the volume of collected speeches on which his reputation for statesmanship rested up to the time of his accession to power. And in order that I may not weaken my case by introducing into it anything hypothetical or uncertain, I have studied to avoid as far as possible imputing to him motives, whether honourable or dishonourable, confining myself entirely to his own recorded utterances, and endeavouring to discover from these alone the methods on which he has proceeded, the range and extent of knowledge or political capacity which he has exhibited, and the qualities by which he has recommended himself to the favour of his admirers and the public generally. But as I desire that my analysis may be as central and thorough-going as possible, and that my own point of view may be made perfectly clear, I have deemed it best to begin by explaining in a word what I mean by the term 'Statesman,' as thereby we shall have found a simple and uniform standard by which his performances, not only in the past but in the future also, may be appraised and judged.

Now perhaps there is no better way of bringing out my meaning than by contrasting with the 'Statesman' the 'Demagogue,' and this contrast again will become all the more apparent if we fix our minds on what to the general public is perhaps a more obvious contrast, viz. that between the scientific physician and the medical quack. The scientific physician differs, one may say, primarily from the quack in this, that he has a distinct *image* in his mind of the various organs, functions, and processes of the body in their relations to one another and to the whole, both in health and disease, and, like the engineer with his engine, in the event of any one part or function becoming disordered or thrown out of gear, sees at once how it will affect all the other organs or functions, and knows in consequence where and how to apply the remedy. The quack, on the contrary, has no such image or knowledge of the parts and functions of the body and their relations to one another; but as he must somehow get credit for this knowledge before he is called in to prescribe, he is obliged to resort to all those arts and expedients by which confidence is inspired, and the appearance as distinct from the reality of knowledge is attained. Hence, instead of relying mainly (as the scientific physician does) for his success on his knowledge of the *facts* with which he has to deal, the quack relies on those merely personal *arts* by which confidence is inspired—the high pose, the mingled air of dogmatism and reserve, the sublime affectation of scorn for the humbler and more laborious methods of the scientific physician (I have known a quack who professed to know all about your inside by merely looking at your eye), and the like. Now if we keep in view this difference between the methods of the physician and the arts of the quack, we shall be able at once to distinguish between the methods of the true statesman and the arts of the political impostor and demagogue.

The first and all-important object of the Statesman, as of the Physician, is to obtain a true knowledge and image of all the *facts* of the body politic with which he has to deal,—economical, financial, industrial, foreign,—and to attain to such a height of vision that he shall be able to see them all clearly as in a bird's-eye view, in their connections, dependencies, and relations to one another and to the whole. The Demagogue, on the contrary, like the quack, having as such no wide knowledge of facts, or central point of view, is obliged to rely for success on certain *arts* or *tricks* which simulate knowledge, and which, as we shall presently see, unless specially safe-guarded against, pass with the unreflecting for wisdom. Bearing this distinction in mind, if we run along the great statesmen of the past, whom all parties alike delight to honour, we naturally alight on the great name of Burke as a typical representative of a statesman of the first order, and although all his speeches bear more or less closely on the special political problems of his own day, the most cursory perusal will show in abundance on every page the two great characteristics of the practical statesman, viz. an intimate and minute knowledge of the *facts* with which he is dealing, in all their variety, complexity, and detail, and a point of view in regard to them so central and commanding that their relations, connections, and dependencies are so clearly seen as in a manner practically to exhaust their purport and significance.

Now if we turn for purposes of comparison from the speeches of Burke to those of Lord Randolph Churchill, we shall see that while Burke's bear all the marks of the true statesman, Lord Randolph Churchill's bear all the marks of the demagogue or political impostor. I have gone through them most carefully over and over again, with the object of seizing if possible their main characteristics, and as result I find that they are all consciously or unconsciously constructed on a few leading arts or tricks, if I may be permitted to call them so, tricks which, although they bear the same relation to the legitimate methods of the statesman as the arts of the quack do to the methods of the physician, nevertheless by the illusion and glamour they create, exercise, until they are ticketed and exposed, a vague but potent influence over the minds of men. With the reader's indulgence, therefore, I propose to examine and expose these tricks separately and individually, and by lifting them high into the light, hope to make it more easy to guard against them in the future.

The first and most characteristic of the tricks on which these speeches are constructed, and the one which obtrudes itself on one's notice so persistently from page to page as almost to shut out all else, is the cheap but ever-effective trick of the Old Bailey barrister, whereby instead of dealing with the simple *facts* and their bearings and relations (in which alone, as I have said, true statesmanship consists), he deals with the *persons* who are engaged on the facts, and makes abuse or criticism of them stand for insight into and grasp of the facts themselves. Now although to men of any penetration this is one of the poorest and sorriest of expedients, it nevertheless is one of mighty potency with the multitude of all classes and ages (who love to see facts through the medium of persons rather than in their abstract nakedness, just as they prefer human life when exhibited in novels and biographies rather than when expounded in abstract philosophies), and unless ruled out as irregular by an intelligent and vigilant Press (as the bombast and irrelevancy of the barrister is by the vigilant judge), will steal in insidiously, and before you are aware of it will have drawn away the allegiance of men. Most of the real work of practical politics, if we consider it, deals with dry and uninteresting facts, great Saharas of statistics and reports and details, which in themselves can be of little or no interest to any human soul, except perhaps to ministers and officials who are charged with them, and who are bound in one way or another to master them. Consider, for example, the question of County Local Government, with its over-lappings and intersections of vestries, poor-law boards, highway boards, quarter-sessions, and the like, in all their confusion and complexity, and say whether in an age when readers can scarcely be tempted beyond a novel, a biography, or a history, any human being would, if he could avoid it, take off his coat to descend into such a cave with the object of evolving if possible order out of its chaos, unless either from a sense of duty, or from the power and honour which the control and mastery of these obstinate and reluctant details would bring him. Not even Sir Charles Dilke himself, with all his acknowledged mastery of the subject, could keep his bored and wearied audience from falling asleep while he expounded it. How easy and pleasant therefore (but also how unprofitable) were it, if instead of having yourself to strip and clean out this Augean stable, you could get as much credit by standing kid-gloved by, and pouring vitriol and abuse on the head of the unlucky statesman who was attempting to grapple with the work, amid the plaudits of the amused spectators. This trick of *Personality*, as we may call it, was a favourite one, as I have said, at the Cogers' Hall, where I have watched it played off with success night after night, and always to the vast entertainment of the miscellaneous audiences that congregated there; one poor man in particular, who was really a master of certain aspects of our political, economical, and financial affairs, being so set upon by the lighter and more superficial newspaper wits and orators, and so pelted, ridiculed, and flaunted for his devotion to his statistics and details, that his very excellences were made to appear to his discredit and almost to his shame.

Now, it was chiefly on this trick of standing aside and indulging in abusive personalities on the ministers charged with the knotty facts involved in practical legislation, that Lord Randolph Churchill relied when he set out with the fixed and deliberate intention of conquering Parliament and the country. Instead of grappling with the *facts* of his opponents directly, as he would have been obliged to do if he had been seated around a table of business-men, with no public out of doors on the *qui vive* for his abuse, or bored House of Commons longing to be roused from sleep or ennui; instead of showing by a larger acquaintance with the principles, complications, or details of his opponent's policy that it was illusory, short-sighted, or grasped with insufficient power, he relied, as I shall show, for his success, on abusive personalities, on blowing out the mental and moral features of his opponent until he got them to that size, angle, or point of distortion where he could dance round them, knocking them about, amid the exultation of his followers, as boys do the stuffed effigies around the bonfires on Guy Fawkes' night; the Press in the mean time, instead of ruthlessly suppressing his personalities as foul, publishing them in all their plenitude and verbosity to whet the appetites of its readers at the breakfast-table; and the populace, instead of, as Carlyle would have recommended, "drumming the ring-leader out and flinging dead cats after him," lifting him on a pedestal to the chair of honour. Not that personal characterization is not at times a most legitimate instrument for laying bare the truth, more especially when it is employed as a symbol or visible image of your opponent's deeper qualities, of his real limitations in insight or habits of thought. Lord Beaconsfield, who if he was distinguished for one quality more than another was distinguished for insight into and contempt for conventional illusions both in politics and society, used this weapon of personality at times with great and legitimate effect. But it was employed by him, and is always applicable, rather to those higher aspects of politics and administration where insight into men is required, than to ordinary legislation, where a knowledge of mere external detail—land tenures, local government boards, and the like—is chiefly necessary and valuable.

But this high, subtle, and refined form of personal characterization is a fine art in itself, demanding as it does some of the finest qualities of the intellect, and to it Lord. Randolph Churchill is a stranger. He has not the power of shading or graduating the expression of his thought so that it shall be a faithful mirror or image of the persons or facts; nor indeed for his purposes was such a power necessary. A broader and less refined form of characterization is all that is required of the demagogue who appeals to the great multitude,—what may be called the Circus-canvas Style of political portraiture, where the colours are laid on in thick, gaudy, glaring masses of light and shade, without gradation, subtlety, or truth; and where the picture exceeds as much in demoniac darkness, ferocity, or beauty the real person portrayed, as the paintings on the circus-canvas do the animals or men within. For with the careless and inartistic public (as with children) on the look-out for excitement and amusement, these daubs and caricatures serve their purpose admirably, and excite more wonder, awe, and admiration than the literal truth would do; and in democracies therefore you may confidently predict that they will cease to be employed by the demagogue only when their counterparts on the circus-canvas shall cease to be employed by the enterprising Barnums of the future. But as in Party Government the latent antagonism and passion secretly felt by the opposing parties (owing to their real divergencies of interest) are easily blown into a flame, political success, you will find, attends the steps not of the genial and kindly political caricaturists,—the Sir Wilfrid Lawsons of debate,—who, although amusing, are too humourous and gentle to arouse political passion (the secret object of all party agitation), but of the virulent and abusive firebrand—the Pawnee who brandishes his tomahawk with the intention of taking scalps, and who can excite hope or fear in consequence in the breasts of friends or foes. This is the man who in Party Politics tends to become a political power when governments approach a democracy, more especially in the party whose future outlook is to fight a losing battle. In the days before the first Reform Bill, when the People could scarcely be said to be represented in Parliament at all, the virulent demagogue was to be found chiefly among the disfranchised classes; the aristocratic members of the House, on the other hand, being in style and manner conspicuous models of courtesy, moderation, and dignity. But now that the cause of the People is everywhere triumphant, the Privileged Classes, who are everywhere fighting at a disadvantage, want not the light and genial, but the abusive and rancorous leader, and are prepared to reward him when found with authority, place, and power; the People, on the contrary, having become by victory and success so careless and relaxed, that I personally shall not be surprised (unless indeed the Press in the mean time should take upon itself once more its true office of winnower) to see before long the political *raconteur*, the joker, and after-dinner speaker seated in the chair of state.

Now Lord Randolph Churchill having thrown in his lot with the classes who are fighting a losing battle, and feeling himself " expected," as he says, " to garnish his speeches with every variety of vituperation," adopted in his personalities (and that too as much from the limitations of his mind as from personal choice) not the genial style of the kindly political humourist, but the ruthlessness of the Pawnee clothed in the language of the *Western Editor*—a style of political warfare long since extinct in all civilized assemblies, and to be met with in its perfect form only in the newspaper controversies of rival editors in the backwoods of America. The advantages of this style are, that it is always effective in a Democracy when it can reach the People through the Press, and that, like highway robbery, it is open to the capacity of the meanest intellect stimulated by ambition or greed, and unrestrained by conscience or heart. All you have to do is to take a dictionary, and for shot and ammunition make a collection of all the long-winded and abusive adjectives expressive of personal or moral reprobation you can find, fire one or other of these at your opponent on every occasion on which you have to mention his name, and the thing is done. Lord Randolph Churchill accordingly, as I have said, adopted this style as at once effective and within the limited scope of his powers, and his speeches in consequence abound in superlative epithets drawn from the utmost range of the personally and morally repulsive. By his language alone, and his epithets applied to his opponents (which are laid on thick with the big brush and in the sign-board style), you will almost know him anywhere out of the said backwoods of America. As samples of what I mean, take the following cheap phrases which he applies to his political opponents, all, the reader will observe, in the moral superlative—'venomous,' 'remorseless,' 'blatant,' 'flagrant,' 'squalid,' 'renegade,' 'bloodthirsty,' 'nefarious,' 'baneful,' 'prodigious,' 'audacious,' 'treacherous,' 'ineffable,' 'awful,' 'tremendous,' 'immense,' and the like.

By way of illustrating these poor tricks on which his speeches are constructed, and by which he rose to his present position, I determined to mark a few passages (from the printed speeches I have mentioned) for quotation, but so thick and fast did they fall under my pencil as I went along, that I was obliged to select only a few of the more typical, by way of making my meaning more clear to the reader. If it be urged that these are matters of style rather than of substance, I reply that it is just one of those cases where the style is the man, and the whole man. These tricks are the very staple and body of his speeches; there is no substance in them beyond this; the thin and watery show of thought and argument running through them being, as I shall demonstrate farther on, so poor and unsubstantial as not to be worth mentioning. And yet in adducing even the following few quotations, I feel I am trespassing on the reader's indulgence, and must apologize to him for resurrecting passages of so little intrinsic worth from those faded controversies which are as uninteresting now as the old newspapers in which they lie entombed. My only excuse for venturing to ask the reader to accompany me through these quotations is the hope that we may so truly seize the round and scope of his mind, as to be able to base on this knowledge some solid generalizations for the future. Now in these passages which are typical of his general manner, you have the tricks of the demagogue which I have just exposed, mingled and united in all combinations; sometimes the *personality* striking you most forcibly, sometimes the *caricature* and *exaggeration*, sometimes the use of the *moral superlative*, and again the *war-paint* of the savage.

Here are a pair of portraits of Mr. Bright and Mr. Gladstone, for example, in the circus-canvas style, which fairly represent the sort of thing by which Lord Randolph Churchill has climbed to be a minister of the Crown. The reader will especially observe in his choice of epithets the free use of what I have called the 'moral superlative.' Of Mr. Bright he says, "The savage animosity which Mr. Bright has breathed into his speeches has raised a corresponding spirit among his opponents. The robe of righteousness with which he and his confederates have clothed their squalid and corrupted forms shall be torn asunder, naked and ashamed shall they be beheld by all the intelligent public, and all shall be disclosed which can be, whether it be the imposture of the so-called people's tribune, or the grinding monopolies of Mr. Chamberlain, or the dark and evil deeds of Mr. Schnadhorst" (Woodstock, 1884). Again, of Mr. Gladstone he remarks, that "from the disastrous day on which he shattered Arabi till now he has wandered amid the devastation purposeless and bewildered, has made no effort to relieve from their burdens the Egyptian people; but haunted and distracted by the guiltiness of his intervention, he has added misery to misery and woe to woe, till he has transformed the fair land of Egypt into a perfect hell upon earth" (Blackpool, 1884).

In the following, again, you have the war-paint laid on thick and strong. After describing the Liberal ministry in power as having " on their souls the blood of the massacre of Mainwand, the blood of the massacre of Lang's neck, the blood of Sir George Colley, the blood of Lord Frederick Cavendish and Mr. Burke, and many other true and loyal subjects of the Crown in Ireland, the blood of Hicks Pasha and his 10,000 soldiers, the blood of the army of General Baker, the blood of Tewfik Bey and his 500 heroes," he goes on to say, "For four years this ministry has literally waded in blood; their hands are literally dripping and reeking with blood. From massacre to massacre they march, and their course is ineffaceably stamped upon the history of the world by an overflowing stream of blood." (Woodstock, 1884). Of the colleagues and supporters of the Liberal Leader, he says, " These parties have so wallowed in a stifling morass of the most degraded and servile worship of the Prime Minister, that they have sunk below the level of slaves; they have become mere puppets, the objects of derision and contempt; they have lost all claim to the title of Englishmen, and I think they have lost all claim to the title of rational human beings" (Piccadilly, 1884). And almost on every page you come across such deep-dyed patches and daubs as the following, and all, as you will observe, in the moral superlative:—'gangs of political desperadoes,' 'legions of foul fiends,' 'corrupt and filthy dynasties,' 'most desperate instincts of the human race,' 'ill-omened and sinister machinations,' 'unmasked impostors,' 'poltroons and traitors,' 'prodigious imbecility,' 'transparent humbug,' 'public malefactors,' 'evil and moonstruck minister,' 'purblind and sanctimonious Pharisee,' and the like.

And it is for such stuff as this, which let the reader decide whether in the open market it cannot be turned out by the ream for a penny a line, and which I will myself undertake to supply from the Cogers' Hall in unlimited quantities for a pot of ale, that a man (with the Press to advertise it and blow it round the world) may become Leader of the House of Commons, and possible Prime Minister of England!

But the Demagogue, when for any reason he cannot venture safely on blowing out the mental or moral *features* of his opponent until they become caricatures, can always exaggerate or distort his policy and *facts;* and so get them at that angle where they will afford matter for abuse or ridicule according as circumstances or the exigencies of party warfare may demand. Now this too, like the circus-canvas style of personal portraiture, is at once the lowest and easiest kind of political criticism, and Lord Randolph Churchill in consequence was not slow to adopt it; the two together making up almost the entire body and staple of his political utterances. It is, as I have said, one of the cheapest of tricks, all you have to do being to represent your opponent's mole-hill of fact as if it were a mountain, or his mountain as a mole-hill, when the policy of course which is naturally adapted to the one will show disproportioned and absurd when applied to the other. Or again, if your opponent has fairly adapted his means to his ends, or to the obstacles to be overcome or passed, you have only to blow up his gnat to the size of a camel, and then by demonstrating how impossible it is for this camel to pass through the eye of the needle which was to receive it, you make your opponent appear like a fool or worse, and yourself remarkably clever. It is in the field of Foreign Policy especially that this poor expedient of the demagogue is most available, and can be played with the least danger of immediate detection. What with the ignorance of the general public in reference to all matters of external policy, and the want of the minute diplomatic knowledge necessary to understand the action of the ministry in power, what with the sensitiveness of the nation at home, and the necessity of walking warily so as not to give needless offence to foreign Powers, Foreign Politics is the very harvest-field of the political impostor; as that class of medical cases where the prejudice or ignorance of the patient unites with the obscurity of the disease is the very field for his medical prototype. Here you can pose, exaggerate, bully, or denounce at will, without let or hindrance, and with the least danger of exposure. Lord Randolph Churchill with the true eye of the demagogue perceived this, and instead of seizing the large scope and intention of his opponent's policy, and dealing with that by a larger perception of its legitimate effects; instead of allowing for the way in which this policy has to be deflected, as in a game of chess, by unforeseen circumstances; he sits over each separate incident and detail, and like that countryman who went to hear Paganini play, and brought away with him only the number of times the great virtuoso's elbow moved during his performance, he counts the number of separate incidents and details, exaggerates these into separate policies (much as if he were to represent the separate moves of a great general as separate campaigns), and because he cannot find in the separate details the unity that he might expect in the whole policy, he holds them up for ridicule or reprobation. He discovers, for example, eighteen different policies of the Government in Egypt, and ten different policies in Ireland, and like those old gossips who give an appearance of credibility to their exaggerations and romancings by affecting to give them precision and circumstantiality, he enumerates these different policies in detail, giving them each secretly, however, at the same time just that little jog of exaggeration necessary to throw them out of the line of their true course and reason, thus making the whole seem to reel as in a drunkard's dream. And having in this way torn up the separate rails on the line and placed them more or less at angles to each other, he then takes the high pose, and asks you to observe how absurd it was for his opponent to imagine that he could run a connected train of policy over them. He drugs the facts, poisons them with exaggeration, and then asks you to observe their absurdity.

Now this poor and miserable expedient of giving his opponent's facts just that little or greater push from the actual truth which will enable him to throw vitriol on them (for of genial humour in all this long desert there is none) is of the very essence of the procedure by which he has raised himself to power, and marks the main characteristics of his mind. Through all his speeches runs this continuous thread of exaggeration and misrepresentation, consisting generally in broad obtrusive exaggerations, but sometimes being seen rather in omission than in commission. He leaves out the qualifications by which his opponents have hedged their general principles; he dilates the part to the dimensions of the whole, or contracts the whole to part; and by the free use of his war-paint and the 'moral superlative' generally, makes his criticisms almost useless except for the lowest party ends. Not only does he do this from choice, but from the natural limitations of his mind he is obliged to do it, or he would have little or nothing to say. For if you can measure a man's intellect as you can an artist's ability, by the power he has of so shading the expression of his thought as to make it the exact image of the fact to be represented (exaggeration being the sign of want of intellect, as the violent colours of the daub and sign-board are of the want of art), you may truly affirm that Lord Randolph Churchill has no other resource to keep him going than some more or less mingled and combined forms of personality, exaggeration, and abuse. If it be true that a Burke could see in the simplest political facts, real relations and connections of such ever-widening scope and complexity as would fill many speeches, it may be said of Lord Randolph Churchill, that without the opportunity of 'scoring' which in Party Governments personality, caricature, and pose afford him, he would come to a standstill altogether. Here, for example (and by way of illustrating my meaning), are a few instances of the kind of exaggeration of which his speeches are composed; and you will observe that when the exaggerations in each are cut down to something like the measure of truth, the propositions become platitudes, without meaning, instruction, or point. "The Liberal Party of the present day has not one single common principle of policy either in home or foreign affairs on which for purposes of efficient government it can unite even for a day" (Blackpool, 1884). Of the Crown, Lords, and Commons, he says, "The Radicals tell you that these institutions are hideous, poisonous, and degrading, and that the divine caucus is the [only machine which can turn out, as if it were a patent medicine, the happiness of humanity" (Blackpool, 1884). Again of the Liberal Government he says, "Talk of Bulgarian atrocities, add them together, and even multiply them if you will, and you will not exceed the total of the atrocities and the infamies which have distinguished with an awful repetition the most blood-stained and withal the most cowardly government which England has ever seen" (Piccadilly, 1884). Of the same Government he further remarks,—"I know that Her Majesty's Government have a great and ineffable contempt for the House of Commons, and if it is any satisfaction for honourable gentlemen to know,

I might say that the House of Commons have the same contempt for them" (House of Commons, 1884). And again of the Radical party he says, "In its blind and unreasoning fury against political opponents it has finally and forever lost whatever of truth and what little of patriotism it ever possessed" (Birmingham, 1884). Of the condition of our industries in 1884 he remarks,—"Your iron industry is dead, dead as mutton; your coal industries, which depend greatly on the iron industries, are languishing; your silk industry is dead, assassinated by the foreigner; your woollen industry is *in articulo mortis*, gasping, struggling; your cotton industry is seriously sick" (Blackpool, 1884). And so on throughout.

But as these tricks of Personality and Exaggeration (all, as the reader sees, in the circus-canvas style and in the moral superlative) would in themselves have been insufficient for his purposes, and would have been detected and exposed, they had to be supplemented by a third, which was necessary to cloak his real ignorance, and would stand in place of true knowledge, and which indeed is of as much service to the political as to the medical quack,

—the trick, I mean, of *Superior Pose*, whereby you assume that your opponent's facts, methods, and details are on quite an inferior plane to your own, and are to be slighted in consequence as altogether beneath your point of view. For, as we have seen that it is essential to the medical quack that he should affect to despise the physician's patient and laborious methods of scientific observation and experiment, and with his eye-glass pretend to read your inside at a glance by his superior intuition; so the political quack, who is cunning enough to know that the genus 'Statesman' may range all the way from the scope and policy of a vestryman to the high political and philosophic wisdom of a Burke, finds it one of his most efficient resources to take his stand on the plane above you, and pose there as if the facts which seem to you so essential and important are not necessary to his superior intuition and penetration; thus justifying his ignorance of detail by the assumption of a greater range of thought and a higher rank in the scale of statesmen. And yet this most poor and patent device, which one would have imagined would have been hooted down at its very inception as an insult by a body of gentlemen supposed to fairly represent the intelligence of the country, was seized on by Lord Randolph Churchill, and played off with cool and consummate impudence before the House and the Country with as much success and as little suspicion of imposture as if we had been a nation of Yahoos. Take, for example, one or two instances as specimens. In the last parliament of Lord Beaconsfield, Mr. Sclater Booth had introduced a Bill dealing with Local Government, a Bill involving of necessity a vast multiplicity of detail, such as could only be within the reach of Government officials having access to full sources of information. Lord Randolph Churchill, who had already been in the House nearly four years, but had only spoken once before, showed, as might have been expected, as little knowledge of the subject in its entirety (and had indeed almost as little opportunity of knowing) as a boy in the street. But with the instinct of the *poseur* looking out for an opening, he seized the opportunity thus afforded him of playing off on the House this trick of superior pose. He characterized the Bill of Mr. Sclater Booth as ' Brummagem stuff,' and as "stuffed with all the little dodges of a President of the Local Government Board when he came to attempt to legislate upon a great question;" ending by remarking, "I have no objection to the President of the Local Government Board dealing with such questions as the salaries of Inspectors of Nuisances, but I do entertain the strongest possible objection to his coming down here with all the appearance of a great law-giver, to repair according to his small ideas and in his little way breaches in the British Constitution." There you have the trick of Superior Pose complete, played openly and without disguise; and with such *éclat* and success that the Editor of his speeches (now the Editor of the *Daily News*) bent before it in good faith (especially before the last sentence) as before a stroke of genius. Or take again the late Egyptian expedition, and mark the superior pose in the ease with which this Bobadil of politics would have settled the difficulty. To arrest the Mahdi, he says, "All that was necessary was a slight movement of troops, a small equipment, a little more energy, a little more precision, a little more common-sense, a little more consistency in your foreign despatches, and the thing is done."

Now I have known men whose dislike of being practised upon was so strong that they would virtually find ground for quarrel in a straw rather than be 'taken in'; but that this poorest of tricks, which I have seen played off night after night at the old Cogers' Hall until one blushed at it, should be swallowed by the public without a strain and in all simplicity and good faith, and that as reward for being so practised upon (and with so little discomfort), the dexterous operator should be made minister of the Crown and Leader of the House of Commons would, had it not happened under one's very eyes, have almost surpassed belief.

"But surely," I can fancy the reader exclaiming, "there must be something more than this in a man who has risen to be Leader in the House of Commons and one of the foremost political figures of the time!" Ah, that is indeed the wonder of it, and the pity of it too; and it is precisely because it was by these poor tricks and these alone that he rose to his present position, that I am here to protest against it with all the energy in my power. For, if it be true that a man may rise to power by such arts, we may as well all lay down our pens, close our books, cease from all liberal studies, renounce all high ideals and exemplars, and armed with bludgeons, take to the political highway at once; for if our object be political success, we shall in this way sooner attain it. I have gone through these speeches, I can conscientiously say, with the greatest care, and with the desire of discovering, if possible, any connected scheme of policy, any evidence of genuine penetration, any observation, or series of observations, such as would justify his rise to his present exceptional position; and in firmly declaring that in the long and dreary waste through which I have had to plod, none such appear, my only regret is, that as I cannot quote the whole volume of these speeches, and cannot in consequence prove a negative, I am obliged (while showing what I do find there) to throw on his supporters and admirers the burden of producing such evidences of originality, penetration, or power, if they are to be found. I have looked carefully, for example, for evidence of some wide-embracing scheme of policy in his shibboleth of *Tory-Democracy;* but find it instead to consist, on the one hand, of certain ideas borrowed from the Radicals—on land, education, county-government, Irish affairs, the suffrage, and the like,—ideas which he takes up and lays down again as suits his convenience and designs; and on the other hand, of a defence of the existing British Constitution—Crown, Lords, Commons, and Church,—by precisely the same old arguments which we have seen and heard in Press or on Platform since our infancy,—the Crown on the ground of stability and continuity; the Lords as checks to popular impulse and defence against the one-man-power or demagogue; the Church on the ground of some vague and indefinite good. And so he goes sailing along in glorious unconsciousness of the impossibility in any government where there is only a *limited* quantity of power available, of giving it to one without taking it away from the others; as if you could give the effective power (which the democratic part of his programme implies) to the People, without taking it away from the Crown, the Lords, and the Church, and leaving them standing there like empty clock-cases, dignified, imposing, and useless. I have looked also for evidences of *originality* in these speeches, thinking possibly that I might alight on something which for the moment at least might have seemed to be the words of a new oracle; but after careful searching I have come across only two propositions that in any way lie outside the beaten track,—the one, his proposal to restore Arabi Pasha after his banishment, to the government of Egypt; and the other, his proposal to turn out the then Liberal Government by stopping the supplies! I have looked again for evidences of *elevation, range,* or *comprehensiveness* of political view; but instead of finding them, I constantly come on him turning his eye-glass on some insignificant detail, working at it with a great show of industry, and by laborious calculations appearing to go to the very root of things,—as when he calculated the amount of money that would have to be raised by the county of Norfolk to give every agricultural labourer in it three acres and a cow! I have kept a look-out for any evidences of *initiative;* but except in regard to the above cases of restoring Arabi and stopping the supplies, I have come across only the 'old hat trick,' by which he brings out of the hat what has already been put into it, brings out as an independent policy what has already been put into it by Public Opinion and the Press. On the other hand, I have searched for any *central observations* on human life generally, such, for example, as we so often come across in Burke, —observations which by their deep harmony with the laws of the world and the human mind, and by their bearing on the welfare of societies generally, give evidence of their depth and greatness; but instead of these I meet with mere solemn platitudes, mere 'opinions,' having no deep roots in the subsoil of the mind or the world, and which, like the guesses of the ignorant, may in any given instance be true or false, but can carry conviction only to those whose interest or policy it is to believe them. And lastly, I have watched his *manner* of dealing with the arguments of his political opponents. Instead of taking the method of Burke, viz. of breaking the back of his opponent's policy by swinging it around some more comprehensive scheme, with whose deep ramifications and connections it is shown to be out of harmony, he has resort to all the pinchbeck arts of the attorney and village politician. The first and most prominent of these is to quote contradictory passages from the speeches of your various opponents, and by allowing these to neutralize each other, to claim the field for yourself. Another is to show some contradiction between what your opponent said twenty years ago perhaps, and what he says to-day under widely different circumstances. A third is to attach hypothetical motives to everything your opponent says or does, and to see in everything a manœuvre—a manœuvre to keep in power, or to catch votes, or to prolong debate, or to interpose delays, or the like—and then by professing to expose these manœuvres, to get credit for marvellous subtlety and penetration. And if all these arts fail, and your opponent shows himself steady and consistent in his policy, and does not change, your cue then is to accuse him of being a pedant or *doctrinaire*; while if he alters his procedure with circumstances and occasions, you charge him with being fickle, inconsistent, or irresolute. Now all these are the mere vulgar tricks of the attorney, and have on them the brand of the Demagogue, not the hall-mark of the Statesman; and it is of these, and the like of these, that the thin and flimsy thread of argument which I have admitted to run through many of these speeches of Lord Randolph Churchill is entirely composed. Any the smallest mark of originality, penetration, or power, I must challenge his admirers to produce.

Now if the range of ability which is exhibited in the procedure and methods by which Lord Randolph Churchill rose to power be such as I have described (and if I have not exaggerated), what I have said of him ought to hold good in his *future* as well as in his past career. I have watched the course of political speakers over long periods of time, and have invariably observed that the early characteristics of their style and manner (after the mere nervousness and novelty have worn off)—the relative proportion of thought, insight, imagination, power of expression, and the like, observable in their earliest efforts—were still preserved in their latest. What habit or ability there was at the first of tracing political cause and consequence, that habit or power remains, and may be predicted at the last. What facility and fluency, what range and variety of thought, what brilliancy or subtlety, what flavour and quality of sarcasm, wit, or humour there was in the earliest, the same proportion and admixture may still be seen under the newest conditions. More experience and knowledge of facts a speaker may have, more expertness in the acquired ruses and tactics of the game, more of the little arts of the 'old Parliamentary hand'; but these are only the expansion of old faculties, not the development of new ones; while in his great central method of grasping and handling complicated facts of various orders, in his method of undermining a great subject and getting at its heart, in his natural elevation and breadth of view, no change can be looked for or entertained. The old Burke as a speaker is the same as the young Burke, the old Pitt as the young Pitt, the old Gladstone or Disraeli as the young Gladstone or Disraeli. And even with greater truth, if possible, may this be predicted of Lord Randolph Churchill. Here is a man who entered Parliament at the early age of twenty-four, sat in it dumb (with one or two exceptions) for six or seven years, and when he did speak, exhibiting those characteristics which we have since in his days of notoriety learned to associate with his name. Suddenly, and at the age of thirty-one, he deliberately and with fixed purpose lays himself out, by the expedients I have detailed, to conquer the House of Commons and the Country.

Meeting at the outset with almost universal ridicule and contempt, he still persists, carrying out his favourite but discreditable methods of attack remorselessly and without apology or disguise, and as is so often seen to be the case with the unworthy as well as with the good, succeeds at last. To imagine, therefore, that at his time of life (he is now thirty-seven*) he is likely to spring any essentially new or original faculty or combination of faculties on the world, that in essentials he will be in the future otherwise than he has been in the past, is a dream. It is for these reasons, then, and to give the reader an opportunity of testing for himself whether I have been guilty (as many will suppose) of exaggeration in the foregoing pages, that I am prepared to affirm that the same old combination of tricks which I have endeavoured to expose, and by which he has risen to power, will be seen in his future as in his past career. I am of course well aware of the serious nature of prophecy, and of the great risks one incurs in entering on it, but so great is my contempt for the poor and miserable range of ability which these speeches reveal, that, for my own part,

* Autumn '86.

after what I have said, not to give him or his admirers the opportunity of showing that I am wrong, would seem to me to be a kind of intellectual cowardice; and moreover, I shall be more than rewarded if I can only succeed in getting the public to observe for themselves the cheap tricks and impostures which I have detailed, and which, as I shall show in my next chapter, will, if not exposed and hung up for reprobation, in time deliver us over body and soul to the Demagogue alone. I expect then to find that his political speeches in the future as in the past, instead of being characterized by depth and capaciousness of insight, and a wide and subtle perception of the connection of political *facts* with one another and the whole, will when he is in Opposition (and therefore on the aggressive), be constructed mainly on the same lines of abuse and personality as of old. And further, that instead of producing a really fine and truthful portrait of his opponent, a portrait whose fine shading and gradation will stamp it as a piece of art, you will have the same old sign-board style of portraiture, with the features of his opponents so caricatured and blown out as to be almost irrecognizable; and the whole will then be held up and bespattered (for the amusement of the pit and gallery) with epithets drawn from the repertoire of the *Western Editor*, flung on in great red patches, without decency, discretion, or point — the old stock-in-trade phrases of the demagogue and penny-a-liner, all in superlatives and extremes,—'blatant,' 'mendacious,' 'awful,' 'immense,' and the rest. Nor am I prepared to assert that this is due entirely to a deficiency in *moral sense*, as some might imagine. On the contrary, I affirm that it is due to a deficiency of *intellect*, and furthermore that he indulges in this daubing with the big brush, not so much because it politically pays, as because he cannot, if he would, give to the expression of his thought the shading and delicacy of truth. I can still hear him jolting and rasping along in that Paddington speech, as over boulders and gravel, endeavouring in vain to beat out with his fist some epithet that would express his meaning, but getting no nearer to a decent fit than the helmet of a giant might be if put on the head of a pigmy. And furthermore, I shall predict that when he does leave *personality* aside for the moment, and proceeds to deal with his opponent's *facts* and *arguments*, instead of taking the statesman-like method of lifting them off their existing basis and swinging them around some more central and profound policy, instead of annihilating his opponent by a deeper insight into the legitimate connections and ramifications of his steps, facts, and arguments, he will (to hide his want of real insight) adopt his old and favourite expedient of jogging them each a little from its exact and linear course, and then will call on you to observe how they stagger and reel. And I will go still further, and assert, that when he does undertake to examine the facts fairly and without exaggeration, he will turn over only such superficial and surface aspects of them as lie immediately under his eye (as in his calculations about the three acres and a cow), while their deeper roots and connections remain all unexplored.

But stay! there is another alternative open to him. For although I anticipate that his future procedure will be marked by the same old tricks as his past (though perhaps in new and more judiciously admixed combinations to render them more difficult of detection), it is still open to him, now that by means of these tricks he has raised himself to power, to kick away, if he sees advisable, the base ladder by which he has ascended, and to apply himself to the legitimate methods of the true statesman. In that event I venture to anticipate that his performances, except in so far as they are here or there leavened with the old salt of abuse (which will be in itself a feat for him to avoid), will be as flat and wearisome as the Paddington speech I have already described, as uninteresting to the multitude as the performances of the old parliamentary officials whom by his novel methods of warfare he has succeeded in displacing.

Will he then be a failure? and will his party, when they have had sufficient experience of him, hurl him from his place as a convicted impostor? Those who imagine this, in spite of all that might seem to point in that direction, are to say the least simple-minded. On the contrary, the same arts that have carried him to power will, if judiciously played, keep him there; and whatever befalls, he will flourish more and more. The old circus daubs which so attracted me as a boy are still to be seen to-day long after I have ceased to admire them; the old melodramas still draw crowded houses long after I have ceased to attend; the old music-hall and negro-minstrel songs still hold the field long after I have outgrown them; and when the Barnums of the future cease from their canvas daubs, when melodramas cease to draw, and music-halls and negro establishments close their doors, then will the arts of the Demagogue which I have described, and by which Lord Randolph Churchill rose to power, cease to be admired, and he himself become a superannuation and a failure. Once get a hold on your Party by any means, and it is comparatively easy to retain it. The Party Journals and the general consensus of opinion largely foreshadow the general *outlines of policy*, and the Permanent Secretaries and higher officials can be always relied on for the details. In administration, too, these same secretaries and officials will, if a Cabinet Minister places himself in their hands, keep the most ignorant, reckless, or flighty in the straight path. How great indeed is the part played by these permanent secretaries, and how little knowledge of his own department is required in a Minister of State, the public have little or no conception; but I have it on the best authority, that it is the opinion of Mr. Gladstone himself, with his forty years experience of office, that if you want an administration to work smoothly, you must allot ministers to those departments of which they have the *least* knowledge, in order to prevent friction between them and the permanent officials! The reader will judge therefore whether there is much likelihood of Lord Randolph Churchill, if he chooses to place himself in the hands of those concealed but most potent despots, the permanent officials, becoming a failure from the mere *want* of knowledge or experience. And above all, when the general Press, in a manner which in my next chapter I hope to make visible to the dullest, begins (as I predict it will as sure as gravitation or the return of the tides) to see in the lightest word that falls from him, greater and greater ranges of 'insight,' 'tact,' 'adroitness,' 'political sagacity,' 'happy phrases,' 'capacity for public affairs,' and the like,—the deliberate impostures and unscrupulousness of his rise under which I and others groan being all condoned and forgotten in the general blaze of vulgar success, or even transfigured by it into a kind of virtue in men's memories, and serving as direct precedent, incentive, and even encouragement to the first reckless, unscrupulous, and ignorant adventurer that passes along,— what hope is there of getting rid of him or the like of him in this world?

And now taking my leave of Lord Randolph Churchill, I come to the main design of this work. I should not, metaphorically speaking, have taken off my coat to expose the tricks of this poorest and most transparent of demagogues, were it not that by giving them definiteness and precision, I hoped to fix them more firmly in the public mind; and by enabling the reader the better to realize the weaknesses in our political system which have made it possible for such a man to rise by such arts to such a position of influence and power, to have taken the first steps toward their removal.

In the remaining pages therefore I propose to exhibit these flaws and weaknesses separately and in detail, drawing them out in threads from the complicated warp of our political and social system, and by concentrating attention on them more fixedly, to make a resort in the future to the same tricks as those by which Lord Randolph Churchill has risen to his present pre-eminence, difficult if not impossible.

CHAPTER VII.

THE DANGERS OF ENGLISH DEMO-CRACY.

NOTHING perhaps can better illustrate the fatal influence of a false political method than the continued existence and vitality of the old political fallacy, that because throughout recorded History, from ancient times downwards, democratic and popular forms of government have ended in anarchy and despotism, therefore they must *always* continue to end so. This fallacy indeed is one which never seems to go entirely out of fashion with journalists, practical politicians, and even political Thinkers; and to this hour it still continues to wave its old ragged, faded, and weather-beaten sides to the wind, as if it were the very emblem of political truth. At the present time the most profound and illustrious, perhaps, of the exponents of this doctrine among political Thinkers is Sir Henry Sumner Maine. This highly accomplished and cultivated Philosopher had already done yeoman's service in the cause of truth by his thorough-going application of the historical method to the phenomena of early societies, and to the existing records of ancient law and custom,—as seen in the old Roman Law, the Brehon Law, and the customs of village communities in the East and West. Accordingly, when it was announced that he was preparing a work on Popular Government, the Press, hushed into a kind of religious silence, awaited his voice as that of an oracle; and when the book at last appeared, so great an effect had the old historical treatment of the question on the graver journalists and publicists, that it was authoritatively announced that a severer blow had here been dealt at the popular confidence in democratic governments than it had ever yet received. Now it so happened, that previously to the publication of this work, I had already, in a book of my own on Civilization, endeavoured to give the *coup de grâce* once for all to this old and superannuated superstition of the hopelessness of Democracy as a form of Government; but on turning to the work of Sir Henry Maine, to my surprise the same old fallacy was borne triumphantly along on the crest of his brilliant and varied argument —an argument based chiefly, as I have said, on historical data, but propped and surrounded here and there by certain shrewd and even profound incidental observations which although giving a show of power and variety to his thesis, were after all but of secondary and subordinate importance. On seeking for the reason of this continued apotheosis by Sir Henry Maine of the old and worn-out fallacy that Democracies must necessarily end in anarchy and despotism, I found it to be due entirely to his false political *method*. Instead of taking his stand on a just insight into the world of To-day, and using historical facts, however true, as illustration and appendage only; he makes History the entire basis and mainstay of his argument, to the disparagement of a just insight into the problem as it stands at the present time. Because, for example, he finds a number of democracies scattered up and down the pages of History—Rome, Greece, Italy, France, South America,—and because, on following their course he finds that they all have gone the same road through anarchy and despotism onward to destruction, he concludes that all *future* democracies must follow the same course. He might as well indeed have argued that because certain trees have not flourished on certain soils, they will not flourish on any soil. For democracies, like trees, have a vital principle as well as an environment in which they are planted; and no merely historical method of argument (proceeding as it does on concrete instances where both *vital principle* and *surroundings* are lumped together) can give us the least insight into their *future* destinies when placed under other and more favourable conditions. For if you have planted a democracy on an unfavourable soil and amid unfavourable surroundings, and it decays and dies, you have still (before the fact can be of any use to you for future guidance) to inquire whether its death was due to its unhappy conditions and surroundings, or to the weakness, falseness, or impotence of the democratic principle itself—quite a different matter. Now in my work on Civilization already alluded to, I have shown that in the instances in which democracies have failed in ancient and modern times, the failure has been due to their *conditions* of existence rather than to the *principle* of Democracy itself. I pointed out, for example, that among the main causes of the downfall of the Roman Republic was the *institution of Slavery;* that this institution working with other economic causes led to the expropriation of the smaller landed proprietors, and the cultivation of large tracts of country in consequence by great gangs of slaves; that this again brought about a great concentration of power in the hands of a few wealthy patricians, and led to the crowding of the expropriated proprietors into the city, where they soon became a hungry and dissolute mob, lending themselves to the quarrels of rival patricians, and willing for 'bread and the circus' to sell their allegiance to the first passing adventurer. I pointed out also that the downfall of the old democracies of Greece was due largely to their *smallness of size,* whereby the whole people could take part in every smallest act of administration however delicate or important, thus laying themselves open to anarchy and corruption on all hands, and to the chance, nay to the certainty, there is in all large public assemblies of being led away by envy, hatred, cupidity, vanity, jealousy, or revenge. Besides, the republics both of Greece and Rome were *warlike,* and liable in consequence to destruction by other Powers; War itself was a necessity inherent in the very age and circumstances of the world, when boundaries were uncertain, prescription had not attained the force of right, and successive hordes of barbarians rendering all unsettled, kept swarming into the sunny lands from the surrounding darkness. And when one empire rose after another out of the chaos, and Rome at last conquered the world, the necessity of keeping the peace among so many tributary and mutually hostile states, and of protecting the provinces from spoliation by her own rapacious patricians, of themselves necessitated the deposition of supreme power in one single despotic hand. It is the same too in Modern Times. Slavery, as all know, came near to wrecking the great American Republic in our own time. The fall of the first French Republic was due largely to the excessive *centralization* of the government which had come down from the old despotic *régime*, and which when war made concentration necessary, lent itself with the greatest ease to the ambitious designs of the military usurper. And the present French Republic is still unsteady, owing chiefly to the old relics of Feudalism, Catholicism, Militaryism, and Caste, which still mingle with the strictly democratic elements of Science, Industry, and Peace.

Now the above, which were all main causes in the decline or fall of the democracies of the ancient and modern world, lay, as is evident, in the unfavourable *conditions* of soil and environment in which these democracies were planted, rather than in the essential *principle* of democracy itself. If therefore ancient democracies perished from *slavery*, why should modern ones fall, now that slavery is everywhere abolished? If they perished from their *smallness of size* and the direct intervention of the people in every act of administration, why should modern republics which are large and are governed only through the system of representation, go the same way? If from *war*, unsettlement of boundaries, and absence of prescriptive rights, why now, when every day prescription becomes more binding, boundaries more defined, and war in consequence more remote? Or if from excessive *centralization*, why now, when the tendency is everywhere to local self-government? Or from the *conflicts of interests and sentiments* caused by Militaryism, Feudalism, and Caste, when every day brings us a step nearer to the reign of Science, Equality, Industry, and Peace?

But if ancient and modern democracies, then, have fallen rather from the unfavourable conditions of the soil in which they were planted, than from the inherent viciousness of the principle of Democracy itself; and if these unfavourable conditions are to a large extent absent in our own time, or are becoming day by day less dangerous, we have still to inquire whether (as the political millennium has not yet arrived) there are any conditions *at present* existing in English Politics which would tend to make the practically democratic *régime* under which we are now living dangerous or unsteady; and if so, whether any natural checks are to be found which if recognized and applied would neutralize, limit, or entirely remove the dangers to which from these unfavourable conditions we are exposed.

Now to answer these questions aright, we have first to ask whether there is anything in our *foreign* relations which, by the dangers to which it would expose us in the event of war, would, if not threaten our existence as a nation, make grave alterations in our constitution a necessity? and secondly, whether there are any great natural cleavages of interest, sentiment, or condition *among our own people themselves* which, like the antagonism of interest and sentiment between the North and South in America before the Civil War, are in danger of being so strained as to make anarchy a possibility, or a restriction of liberty inevitable?

In answer to the first of these questions—viz. as to our Foreign and Colonial relations—it is enough to say that England is an Imperial and European power, to make (at the first blush) her need of a steady and concentrated executive, and her unsuitability for government by a democracy dependent on parliamentary majorities, apparent. And yet on further inspection, this fact of our being an Imperial and European Power (which to most other European States would spell ruin if under a democracy), although at critical times always a possible source of danger, is not in a general way really so dangerous as would at first sight appear. In the first place, England herself being an insular Power, and practically safe from attack behind her wooden walls, is free from the dangers to which all other European States (having frontiers to defend) are liable. In the second place, her Colonies are practically self-governing, and most of them, as so happens, lie in quarters of the world where the chances of quarrels which might lead to serious collisions with other States are few and remote; while the government of our Indian Empire being left mainly (except perhaps in reference to foreign affairs) in the hands of the Governor-General and his Council, is thereby taken out of reach of the shifting and unsteady control of party politics, and governed on the spot as its safety or necessity dictates. In answer to the second question, as to whether there are any causes of conflict or antagonism among *our own people themselves* which might prove to be sources of danger, the first thing that strikes one, leaving Ireland out of the question, is the sudden implanting of an essentially full-blown democracy on a soil still largely feudal both in its tenure of land and its material and social conditions. Now, to believe that a Democracy with full political power will not strive slowly or quickly to realize its own strength, aspirations, and ideals, and at the expense, if necessary, of the owners of the soil or the wealthy capitalists, to carve out for itself a state of society in its own image and interests, is simplicity. And yet, on the other hand, to imagine that these same landowners and capitalists who at present possess (and can handle and control as they please) the accumulated wealth of the soil and of industry, will allow this wealth to be filched away from them without a struggle, by the incantation over them of a few fine phrases about 'the rights of labour,' 'the rights of the people,' and the like, previous to these phrases being solemnly turned into legal enactments, is even a greater simplicity. Hence, during the struggle, be it swift or be it gradual, one might expect a period of great tension and antagonism between the propertied classes generally and the great body of the people. And as all see that the struggle is sooner or later inevitable, the answer to the question whether it will be gradual and healthy, or swift and revolutionary, whether wise and moderate, or reckless and anarchic, whether the State will bear up gaily against the strain, or relax towards anarchy and despotism, will depend entirely on *the choice of leaders*. Whether you shall strain the cohesion and stability of the State by the antagonism and passion that must inevitably be aroused by any sudden attempts of the masses to realize their ideals, either by the expropriation of landlords or by socialist violence; or whether, on the other hand, you shall accommodate opinion and sentiment to necessity by a series of gentle gradations (something in the manner in which the Crown has been smoothed gradually into acquiescence with the will of the people by the gradual derogation of power which has taken place from the time of Charles I. to our own day), and all so softly and smoothly, broadening down from precedent to precedent, that nothing seems to have been filched away at all; must manifestly depend entirely on the justice, moderation, and ability of the men whom the different parties will select as their guides and leaders. How much depends on the ability and character of a ruler or leader who has once become accredited, may be seen, in the past, in the lightness with which nations and peoples have followed the most giddy and frivolous of kings into caprices and follies which have ensured their downfall; and in our own day, by the large following admittedly given whether rightly or wrongly to Mr. Gladstone's Home Rule Bill on the mere prestige of his name alone. So supremely important is it, therefore, in the times of tension and antagonism between the various classes in our country that are visibly coming on, whether your leader shall be a Burke or a Lord Randolph Churchill!

For if the danger to the State which must always arise when great and powerful interests and classes stand glaring at one another in fierce antagonism and passion cannot be averted by the wisdom, foresight, and moderation of the men chosen as leaders, how indeed can it be averted? It is hopeless to imagine that once having arrived at the goal of pure democracy you can go back again to a restricted suffrage, or to any form of fancy franchise, plural voting, and the like expedients of other days; there is something in the very genius, impulse, and onward march of the world which forbids the thought in its inception. Democracies must first of all realize in outward fact their inner and essential principle of equality, in every sphere of life, before they can be induced even to look about them for checks to their weaknesses or dangers. It is not likely, therefore, that before they have accomplished their mission they will consent to unseat their dignity by returning to the restricted suffrages and other outworn instruments of the old *régimes*. Nor would it avail them aught if they did. Good government is not to be conjured back again by returning to the limited franchise of select classes, with the selfish class legislation which would return with it as surely as the tides with the moon; nor by any system of handicapping by which power would be thrown into the hands of the educated classes, who, although having sufficient intelligence to see the effects of political measures intended for the benefit of the many, would, when the measures ran against their own interests, be prevented by selfishness from acting up to their insight. As all hope therefore of benefit to be derived from restricting the suffrage is futile, whatever dangers still cling to our democracy in face of the external or internal antagonisms and strains to which it is exposed, must be met, if met at all, in some other way. Now it is the virtue of despotisms and oligarchies, that in the calm discussion of public business around a table, where all mere rhetoric would be an impertinence, where nothing but facts and their significance are admitted, and any unhappy member who should attempt to orate would be immediately gagged, you have a policy of State marked by intelligence, consistency, and continuity; while their vices are their want of morality, and the injustice they habitually do both to persons and classes. The virtue of democracies is that by allowing the free representation of every variety of opinion and interest in their midst, they thereby insure that a general even-handed justice is done to all persons and classes; while their vices, on the other hand, are their muddle-headedness, their want of intelligence, and the absence in them of a continuous and consistent policy. But to imagine, as some do, that democracies will reinforce themselves against their own vacillation and stupidity by renouncing their very essence, viz. equality of conditions, and by a restriction of the suffrage become something else than democracies, that is to say oligarchies, is a dream. If democracies are ever to become safe and efficient instruments of government, it will be not by *renouncing* that which is their special virtue,—equality to all of privilege and right,—but by *adding* on to their own special virtue the virtues of their opponents —viz. intelligence, consistency, and continuity; and this, as I have already said, can only be done by the selection as leaders of wise and good men.

To this one conclusion, therefore, all roads lead. So long as a democracy remains a democracy, a continuous and intelligent foreign policy can only be had, if had at all, by the selection of wise leaders; so long as there is any great antagonism of interest among the various classes of its people, as may be the case with ourselves, this antagonism will not be removed by merely sprinkling rose-water on it, but can be wisely met only by the selection as leaders of men of real insight and character.

The question then arises, whether a democracy can of itself be entrusted with *the choice of wise leaders.* To this I should reply in the negative, and for several very valid reasons. To begin with, I would point out that just as the laws of bodies *in the mass* are different from, but quite as certain as, the laws of the *particles* of which they are composed, so the laws of the action of men when congregated in masses are different from, but equally true with, the laws of their action as individual units. And it is just because of this difference between the action of men in masses and their action as individual units, that democracies are not to be trusted to choose for themselves wise and good leaders. It will, I presume, be generally admitted that what is wanted in a practical statesman is not so much the man who by merely mounting the stump echoes the passions, interests, or desires of a particular class or community, as the man who is equipped with the wisdom and knowledge necessary to carry these desires into wise and legitimate action; just as in a general we want not the man who can shout 'to Berlin,' 'to Moscow,' but the man who can successfully take us there —quite a different matter. Now it is the first law of men when gathered into masses that they tend to select as leaders those who merely *echo* their interests or sentiments, rather than those who know how to *give effect to* these interests and sentiments in wise and harmonious legislation. This holds true from the practised demagogue, who from his choice of phraseology can ring all manner of changes on the prevailing sentiment or passion of the hour, to the ignorant and vulgar demagogue who can but parrot some popular cry, as 'Down with the landlords,' 'Down with the priests,' 'Cheap loaf,' 'Protection for native industry,' and the like. And hence it happens that if among the dead level of heads in a crowd one man can manage to get above the rest so that all eyes can be focussed on him (even if it were by taking advantage of some chance stump, roof-top, platform, or through the columns of a newspaper), and from the point of vantage thus gained, utters what everybody has just been saying in the crowd below, he ceases to be quite the same ordinary man he was a moment before; he becomes surrounded by a kind of lustre which exceeds his own natural lustre as much as the concentrated passion or sentiment of a crowd exceeds that of any individual. And just as men become frightened when they see others frightened, and as the object of their fears assumes an appearance dark and menacing out of all proportion to the reality; so a man whose remarks if made in private would seem only natural, usual, and just what we ourselves should say, seems, when he makes precisely the same remarks in public, and they are heard through the chorus of applause which ascends to him on all sides, suddenly to acquire a new importance and distinction. His very isolation and elevation, and the consciousness that he is the object of a common sentiment and sympathy, surround him with a kind of halo as of a person apart, and he is never again quite the same poor creature he was before. Even a piece of bunting, a banner with an inscription on it, or better still perhaps some mechanical clock-work figure that could be made to shout the sentiment or cry of the moment, one can almost imagine gathering such a halo around it as would lead, if the thing were possible, to its being approached by its devotees, like some heathen god, for advice, consultation, and direction. And when we remember how we look on any one whom we regard with love and admiration as being in some way possessed of a vague and general all-round excellence and superiority, we can easily imagine that whatever the cry may be—'Cheap loaf,' 'Justice to Ireland,' 'Protection for native industry,' 'Chinese Labour,' 'The land for the people,' 'Freedom to oppressed nationalities,' 'Federation of the Empire,' 'Spirited foreign policy,' 'The poor man's beer,' or any other cry however legitimate and right—we shall have a tendency to select the man who has already excited our admiration by his lively *expression* of the sentiment in question, as the man to be entrusted with the work of carrying it into practical effect, however ignorant he may be of political economy, financial knowledge, or any one form of practical wisdom involved. And thus two qualifications which in the nature of things are distinct and separate, become mixed and confounded: the Sentimentalist takes the place of the practical Administrator, the Talker of the Thinker, the Demagogue of the Statesman. Even in large deliberative assemblies like the House of Commons where the questions dealt with are of necessity of the most practical and business-like character, honourable members cannot escape this tendency of men in masses, but, as we have seen, tend to choose the phrase-mongers and echoers of some popular sentiment as their leaders, rather than the men who are known to have the deepest insight and business-like knowledge. It is one of the great and even damnable illusions of the world, and is so deeply ingrained in men when they come together in large numbers, that it is hopeless to imagine they will escape its influence; and is the deep and secret reason why democracies (where the masses in the long run, as having the votes, are all-powerful) cannot be entrusted of themselves with the selection of wise and good leaders.

If the choice of wise leaders is our only hope of salvation in the conflicts both from within and from without that may in future be in store for us; and if democracies cannot, by their very nature (as coming under the law of the action of men in masses, whether in Parliament or acted upon by the Press, or from the Stump), be entrusted with the choice of these leaders; if, moreover, having once given the suffrage to the people we cannot take it away again and place it in the hands of any select class, however otherwise admirable; we have now to inquire *how* these wise leaders are to be chosen, and whether there is any organization at present existing whose proper and essential function it is to stand between Parliament and the Public, and by winnowing out the false and incompetent competitors, to take care that the Commonwealth shall suffer no detriment from the choice of its leaders.

Now in all well-ordered States, and especially in countries like Britain where from time immemorial political changes have been gradually brought about by a kind of evolution (in spite of the fact that a fully developed Democracy has now been planted on a soil still largely feudal in its material and social conditions), a careful inspection will almost always reveal institutions, or the rudiments of institutions, which shall serve as balance and corrective to the special evils and dislocations to which these societies at different periods of their evolution are liable. In looking around among ourselves for the particular institution on which from prescriptive allowance, common consent, and natural fitness the task devolves of selecting wise men for the leadership, one naturally falls on the *Newspaper Press* as the only one available for the purpose. The *Church* cannot do it; for, in the general way, it restricts itself to its accustomed routine of prayer, praise, and the exposition of the Pauline Theology; and when it does interfere in Politics it can deal only with the moral *results* of legislative measures (and even in this, owing to its connection with the State, very tenderly), but can take no part in *the selection of the men* to whom these measures are to be entrusted. *Individual Great Men*, the 'superior persons' at whom the *Times* delights to sneer, cannot do it; and for the very good reason, that they have no influence with the masses, to whom even by name they are mostly unknown; so that when they do occasionally venture to send a communication to the Press on current politics, the Editor is obliged to introduce and explain them to his readers with a pointer, as if they were statues or fossil remains in the British Museum. If the views of the Great Man happen to agree with those of the Editor himself, he is perhaps heralded in this way,—"A letter in our columns to-day from the great Thinker, Mr. Herbert Spencer, lends weight to the opinion we have all along expressed in reference to the," &c. &c.; whereas should they disagree, it will perhaps run somewhat after this fashion—"Our readers will not attach undue weight to remarks contained in a letter in our yesterday's issue from the pen of Mr. John Stuart Mill (of whom perhaps many of our readers will never have heard), when we inform them that he is a mere viewy *doctrinaire*, who by his writings has acquired some influence over certain advanced sections of the Radical Party," &c. Mr. Freeman himself, with all his knowledge of the history of the constitutions of States and the causes and circumstances of their rise and fall, has to complain that what he has to say on current politics falls on ears deaf and unheeding, and has little or no influence on the course of practical legislation. But even were the general public on the watch for the opinion and guidance of what are known as its 'Great Men,' these great men themselves are not always *en evidence*, and indeed are rarely or never to be found when wanted. Where, for example, were Mr. Herbert Spencer,

Mr. Matthew Arnold, Mr. Froude, Mr. Lecky, Mr. Freeman, Mr. Ruskin, Prof. Tyndall, Prof. Huxley, Mr. Frederic Harrison, and the other watch-dogs of society, when Lord Randolph Churchill, by arts such as I have described, was entering the undefended gates, and (beaten up by the drums of the Press) was being borne triumphantly to the citadel on the shoulders of the populace? Where were they? I ask. Silent all, or barking ineffectually into the vacant night—issuing their manifestoes and pamphlets and protestations against some point of policy, foreign or domestic, of the then Prime Minister, all unheeded as they themselves complain. The multitude who had the votes, deceived by the noise and reverberation which the Press and the Music Hall were giving to the speeches and writings of Lord Randolph Churchill (and dazzled by his sign-board style and his free use of the moral superlative), *honestly* believed these speeches to have in them the ring of true genius, and accordingly elevated him to authority and power. The 'Great Men,' on the contrary, knew them to be trash of the cheapest and lowest order such as could any day be had by the ream in the garrets of Grub St. for a penny a line.

And yet, instead of pointing this out to the people, they sat by silently witnessing his shameful rise, or barking their protestations against his opponent into the drowsy night. Had they indeed turned on the impostor, and uniting their voices silenced the drums of the Press, and blocked the triumphal procession while it was yet time, proclaiming aloud the scandal and disgrace of allowing a man to snatch at the highest positions in the State by playing off a few cheap tricks on the ignorant multitude—they might have done the State some service. But to wait until he had seized the prize, and then to begin, as they doubtless will again, barking as before into the empty darkness—issuing again their pamphlets, and manifestoes, and protestations to an unheeding people—and above all, to know with what cynical contempt he will fling these 'unauthorized' impertinences (with a tail of one) into the waste basket!—it is evident there is little hope of the 'Great Men' saving us from the demagogue, or helping us to choose good and wise leaders.

The individual *Constituencies* (as distinct from the democracy in general) cannot help us in the choice of wise leaders; for their choice is restricted to *single* members, and when uninterfered with from without, usually results in the selection of some largest land-owner, brewer, manufacturer, biscuit-maker, or other merely local potentate as their representative in Parliament,—men indeed who, if they sat quietly round a council table and restricted themselves to public business, would have little or no difficulty in selecting the best leaders available among their own numbers, but who unfortunately when they take their seats and form what is known as the *House of Commons*, are prevented from selecting the best men by several very potent influences. What with their time of life, and the nature of their occupations, which render them more or less speech-bound and unfit to address public audiences, more or less wanting in rapidity, vivacity, and literary finish; what with the Press out of doors pressing on them the pretensions of some light buffoon or scurrilous ruffian of debate, who by the report of his speeches at full length has tickled the general ear; what with the bayonets of their constituencies at their back; and more than all with their having to split themselves up into hostile parties when they take their seats; it is evident that they will select as their leader, and carry to the seat of power, not the man with most real knowledge, experience, and judgment (for what is the use of these unless you can keep the House awake?); but either the most impudent and wordy dialectician who will worry and harass his opponents; or the most virulent caricaturist and sign-painter who can excite and interest the mob; or the lightest and most unscrupulous tactician who, like the Canadian lumberman on the St. Lawrence, can keep himself and his party afloat on a rolling log for the longest time and in the deepest waters; or finally (especially if their cause or party is triumphant), the most genial after-dinner *raconteur*, music-hall humourist, or political negro-minstrel. Wise parliamentary leaders, it is true, once accredited could no doubt select good men as their lieutenants, but they have themselves first to be chosen, which is just the problem before us; as it is, they are obliged, as we have seen, to select their lieutenants for the party support they can give them by length or sharpness of tongue rather than for their real worth, and to appoint them to offices (according to Mr. Gladstone) of which they have the *least* knowledge and experience!

If then the Democracy itself cannot be trusted to choose wise leaders, and if neither the Church, the individual Great Men of the country, the Constituencies, the House of Commons, or the Parliamentary Leaders themselves, for reasons which I have just given, are suitable for the function, it is evident that the only accredited organ that can intervene between Parliament and the People to winnow out, expose, and ruthlessly suppress reputations illegitimately won (by the arts, tricks, phrase-mongering, and other irrelevant qualities which I have described), is the *Newspaper Press*. In the first place, it alone has the authority and prestige necessary and equal to the task; in the second, it is the only organization at the present time that really does (whether we will or no) exercise this function of choosing for us our political leaders. In my next chapter therefore I propose first to show the way in which the Press actually fulfils this duty; and next to inquire what the obstacles are which at the present time stand in the way of the proper fulfilment of this its great and essential public function.

CHAPTER VIII.

THE PRESS AND THE DEMAGOGUE.

IN the old days of Aristocratic and Middle-class supremacy, or roughly speaking, from the time of the first Reform Bill till within the last few years, the Newspaper Press performed its essentially public function of ruthlessly purging away all traces of the Demagogue, and of seeing that the State suffered no injury from the choice of ignorant or incompetent leaders, with admirable insight, discretion, and public spirit. During all those years the *Times* was the real maker and unmaker of ministries,—a veritable 'king-maker' in its way,—and as far as was possible under its then more or less restricted conditions, allowed nothing to escape into the general air of public opinion but what had been thoroughly disinfected and purified, and was at least wholesome and innocuous. In those days the great mass of the people were still unenfranchised, all political power centred in the

Upper and Middle Classes, and a small body of aristocratic gentlemen belonging to the great territorial families chose the leaders of their respective parties, uninterfered with from without, from among their own numbers, or from those of the Middle Class in the House allied to them in interest and sympathy. Radicalism was yet but a struggling and despised wing of Liberalism, a kind of poor relation at best, the more aggressive forms of it current in the present day being in the House almost entirely unknown; while outside, it lay around among the unenfranchised classes in a diffused, fermenting, and as yet inorganic condition, giving signs of its presence and activity only by occasional outbursts of Chartism and the like. Under these circumstances, the course open to a great public journal like the *Times* was, although comparatively restricted, simple, direct, and straightforward. The Upper and Middle Classes being in a sense the State (as alone having the votes), all power, political, material, and social, was in consequence centred in the same hands; and as only *political* stability could keep it there, Politics of necessity became the very essence and *raison-d'être* of the paper; all other subjects and interests (all the liberal arts and specialisms, all interests of music, poetry, the drama, and the like) being, with the exception of occasional reviews of important books read chiefly by these same classes, or sports in which they were all interested, either disdainfully patronized from afar, or degraded into small type in some outlying corner of its sheets. In Politics, as it could not *dictate* the choice of leaders (the borough-mongers were still too strong to allow that), its only course was to loyally accept those chosen for it by the great families and their Whig or Tory following, but to *hold the balance evenly* between them; while it slighted or ignored the exponents of the unenfranchised classes, cut their speeches down to a skeleton, and scouted all expression of adverse opinion from outside Thinkers, however eminent or profound, as 'merely literary' or '*doctrinaire.*' And, moreover, as it stretched its authority like a huge canopy over the entire field of journalism, and all the lesser and strictly party journals that lay around it fought in consequence half paralyzed and emasculated under its overwhelming shade, the multitudinous demagogues who were ready at any moment to start up and make themselves the mouth-pieces of the unenfranchised, and who would, if they had had an organ of sufficient influence in the Press, have risen into influence and power, were as hopelessly cut off from political life as if they had been negro orators addressing a white population in the Southern States. But in spite of this narrowness of aim which was a necessity of the age and time, the *Times* did its duty admirably to the Public to whom it addressed itself. It held the balance, as I have said, evenly between the two great political parties in the State, supporting in a general way the government in power in all well-grounded legislation, and although not of itself able to dictate the choice of leaders, took care that when chosen they should fight fairly and with legitimate weapons, admitting in their speeches nothing but well-grounded facts and arguments, and as remorselessly shearing away all mere rhetoric and phrase-mongering as it would have done the political irrelevancies of a mime or circus clown. It stood, in a word, between Parliament and the Public, and by its vast influence lopped away all those arts, tricks, and graces of the mere rhetorician which, however attractive to the multitude, are not statesmanship; much in the same way as a judge stands between opposing counsel and the jury, and rules out in his summing up all those confusing sophistries of counsel and amusing irrelevancies of evidence which, however attractive in themselves, are not vital to the issue, and would, if admitted, defeat the ends of justice. In this way the *Times*, edited and manned by men of really statesmanlike knowledge and insight, did yeoman service to the country for a period of over half a century.

But in the mean time, what with the growth of population, the spread of education, and the increased facilities opened up by steam communication, a *Penny Press* was growing up under and around the huge shade of the threepenny *Times*, and although overshadowed by it, lying more close and immediate to the varied interests, aspirations, and desires of the great body of the people. Instead of making practical politics its entire aim and concern, and ignoring or degrading the varied interests of art, the drama, music, literature, and the like, as the *Times* did; the Penny Press made a point, while remaining still mainly political, of giving full and proportionate importance to these various aspects of national interest and activity. But while lying thus more closely than the *Times* to the different interests of different classes of the people, it lay also, it must be observed, more closely to their immediate *political* interests, prejudices, and passions. It became, in consequence, more distinctly partizan in spirit; and instead of standing as the high impartial censor and judge *over* them, it became the mere agent and reporter *among* them, whose function it was to mirror, put into shape, and faithfully again *reflect* the political prejudices or interests of its clients. And now, for the first time, the Demagogue (who had been kept safely under hatches by the *Times*), by making himself the mouthpiece of neglected or injured interests, and being taken up by the journals which watched over these interests, began to lift his head into public recognition. As time passed, and the franchise was at last extended to the Working-classes, a still further change came over the face of Politics and the Press. By this political innovation the Upper and Middle Classes gradually lost their political supremacy; the *Times* in consequence (being too expensive for the Working-man) was unable to stretch its influence and jurisdiction athwart the whole field of voters; and accordingly, like a judge without jurisdiction over all the parties to a suit, was forced from its former dignified and judicial attitude of high political impartiality, and thrown for support on those Upper and Middle Classes who had been its public and supporters from the beginning. And as these classes became more and more forced into Conservatism as a make-weight against the growing Radicalism of the working-classes and their organs in the Press, the *Times* was obliged to follow in their footsteps, and to gradually transform itself into a mere party organ. The consequence was that it lost its old high tone of dignified impartiality, and its statesmanlike point of view; and as its general sympathies have not since expanded (it still prefers the alderman to the Thinker) its partizanship has gradually deepened, its political views have become narrower, its insight into the whole range of political cause and consequence has become shallower, until now its political leaders are at times as virulent and abusive as those of the veriest old hack in the ranks. All this was of course natural, and could have been predicted *à priori*. But the consequences of it are lamentable, and do not yet seem even to have dawned on the ordinary editor or leader-writer, who, like the light and happy negro on the old plantations, goes dancing and laughing along as if all were sailing merrily on a sunny sea. It does not appear even to have occurred to them that with no *independent* organs of sufficient influence and importance to deal alike with men and measures in a rigorous, statesmanlike, and impartial spirit, the Newspaper Press, Penny and Threepenny alike, has become not the *guide*, but the *slave* of the great masses of political passion, prejudice, and self-interest into which the country is divided; and that the People themselves being left without guidance, like a jury without the impartial summing-up of a judge, are at the mercy of all kinds of special pleaders, charlatans, and phrase-mongers; and (by the law of men in masses which I have before described) are the very slaves, not of those who exercise their intelligence, but of those who tickle their vanity, amuse their dulness, excite their passions, or impose on their credulity or their hopes. And furthermore, now that the People, thus released from all restraint and guidance, insist on taking matters into their own hands, and choosing their own leaders, the Press may be seen consenting to play the part of procuress, and spreading out before them all the manifold attractions of the Parliamentary artistes for their choice, printing the speeches of the favourites at full length,—jokes, epigrams, happy phrases, buffoonery, scurrility, negro-minstrelsy and all; the Leaders in the end being selected, like the favourites at a music-hall, for the interest, liveliness, or titillation of their minstrelsy or song. And when the People at last have made their selection and declared their choice, the Press of either party in its impotence and for its own self-preservation is, as we see, bound to accept the creatures thus thrust upon it; and is pledged under penalties to discover tones of seraphic music as of a Handel or Beethoven, strokes of genius as of a Shakspeare, in the veriest emanations of the tap-room and the music-hall; flaring the author's name around the county like a fiery cross (as we have seen in the case of Lord Randolph Churchill), and summoning men to his allegiance, thus still further heightening and extending his reputation, and fastening him like a halter still tighter and tighter around its own neck, until at last, by the pressure of what is called 'public opinion,' it is forced on its knees before the very over-stuffed image which itself has made. Even the *Times*, which would once have started at the sight of a demagogue, like Brutus at the ghost of Cæsar, now welcomes him (if he is on the right side) with open arms.

And thus it has come about that the Press, which was once the main instrument in defending us from the Demagogue, is now the main instrument in thrusting him upon us; all the virgin conditions for his success lying blown and ripe under the open sky, and ready to be plucked by the first audacious and unscrupulous adventurer that passes along.

If further proof indeed of this were necessary it could nowhere be better found than in the career of Lord Randolph Churchill, a career through which as through a window you can see the very genius of the Press in its relation to Politics and the Public. Instead of hurrying into the dust-bin the speeches of this most poor, harsh, and unscrupulous of demagogues, and disinfecting them before they were carried like a miasma into the general air (for the blasting contagion of his rise will infect the political atmosphere for many a day), instead of incontinently excising his buffooneries, scurrilities, and personalities, as the *Times* in its old days most assuredly would have done, this very Newspaper Press (which in the person of its representatives I have seen responding to toasts drunk in its honour as a public servant) did at the very time that itself admitted that he was not to be taken seriously, seize on and detail at full length his parliamentary vagaries as if they were tales of murder or adultery, placarding the walls of the empire every morning with their advertisement to arouse the dull curiosity of the bored and frivolous multitude and when at last it had made his name a household word, and given him that notoriety which in this world is ninety-nine points of success, when it found it had lifted him to so high a pedestal of importance that it could not take him down again, it bent the knee to him in a kind of Oriental idolatry; and now has the unenviable honour of having foisted on the country a man of whom it may with strict justice be said (for it is within the memory of all), that whatever his *future* may be, and however his procedure may change, he *rose* to power, and that too by the admission of this same Press that helped him there, by baseness and baseness alone.

Such is the Newspaper Press, and such is the way in which, while having toasts drunk to its honour at public banquets for its public services, it has so whetted the appetite of the Public for political scandal and personality, that the arts of the Demagogue, naked and undisguised, have become the surest passports to power.

To this charge, however, which I have deliberately brought against the Press in general of *precipitating* on us the Demagogue instead of *defending* us from him, I desire to make among others one notable exception—and that is the *Spectator*. On this journal has descended the mantle which the *Times*, for reasons which I have given above, was obliged to drop when the franchise was extended to the great body of the people, the mantle, viz. of sobriety of tone; high impartiality and absence of party bitterness; the endeavour, like a wise judge, to place the connections, sequences, and involved results of opposing views fairly before the reader; the exclusion of all mere rhetoric, verbiage, and personality; and the dealing with facts and their import and connections, and with these alone. Unlike the *Times*, however, when in its best days and as a true public servant it held the scales evenly between the old and narrower political divisions of Whig and Tory, the *Spectator* represents the larger aspirations and more advanced political ideas of our own day; and although progressive in tendency, its Radicalism is so Conservative, and its Conservatism so Radical, that it may fairly be said to be, so far as circumstances will allow, a most high and trustworthy example of political impartiality. And further, instead of degrading, like the *Times*, into small print or ignoring altogether all political thought and social activity that cannot cramp itself into the narrow and severely practical limits of the old aristocratic *régime*, it welcomes in its pages thought of all ranges, from the solidly practical beneath our feet, to the point where the ideal of the future becomes for the present the impracticable or *doctrinaire*. Unlike the Penny Press, on the other hand, instead of taking its opinions from the vague and hasty impressions of its readers, it imposes its opinions on them (at least in the first instance) for consideration; instead of dealing largely with personal recrimination and retrospect, it deals with present facts and their inherent tendencies and consequences, and with these only; instead of retailing the impertinences, frivolities, and personalities of the demagogue for the breakfast table, it shears them unmercifully away as irrelevant, dangerous, and misleading; instead of trading on happy phrases, sign-board portraiture, exaggeration, and personality, it leaves them all alike severely alone. A high-toned, serious, and even great journal, which in itself is a political education; and had all the daily papers done their public duty as conscientiously and well, no Lord Randolph Churchill would by playing off on the Public a few poor and wretched tricks have worked his way into power. But unfortunately by that baulking of fate which is always present to prevent trees growing into the sky, or progress over-leaping the element of Time to its millennial goal, this journal, which is a sixpenny *weekly*, is beyond the reach of the great masses who have the votes, and in consequence has almost as little influence over them as if it were buried in the centre of the earth. The result is that the great Public who now control by their suffrages the destinies of the Empire are left entirely without direction or guidance, and are at the mercy of the first political gust that whirls up from the pavement some light irresponsible shaveling to the seat of power.

CHAPTER IX.

THE ILLUSIONS OF THE PRESS.

WE have already seen in a previous chapter that now that we have entered on the era of Democracy, the important point in the event of any extreme danger or antagonism threatening us from within or without is the choice of wise and good men as leaders. We have seen also that democracies when left to themselves cannot be entrusted with the choice of these wise and good leaders, and further, that among ourselves there is at present existing no institution or body of men with the influence, prestige, and authority necessary for the performance of this high function, unless indeed it be the Newspaper Press. On inquiring farther as to how the Press fulfilled this function, we found that instead of standing (in the persons of its various representatives) like flaming cherubim at every portal of State, and relentlessly cutting off the Demagogue and expelling him from positions of power and authority—a function which the *Times* in its old days and under its more limited conditions admirably fulfilled—it had now, owing to circumstances and conditions partly inevitable and partly perhaps remediable, become the very sport and echo of opinion, converting the Empire by means of its great range and influence into a vast auditorium, into which as into some great sounding gallery it shouts the names and performances of the various mimes and play-actors on the political stage (as much for the amusement as for the instruction of the people), until it so far magnifies and inflates their bulk and proportion in the common eye, that the State is literally, and I say it advisedly, at their mercy. But besides the tendency of the Press to thrust the Demagogue upon us, owing to its position in relation to Parliament and the Public of which I have already spoken, it would almost assuredly be bound to do so by reason of certain weaknesses inherent in itself, certain illusions by which it is possessed, and which must be exorcised before it can worthily perform its great and high public function. In this chapter, accordingly, I propose to point out what these illusions are, and in doing so I trust I may not be thought guilty of presumption or impertinence; for in the history of the decline and fall of States it has often been under the ribs of some great and flourishing institution throbbing with life that the germs of future decay have all unconsciously been permitted to nestle. In order then that I may make my meaning the more clear, I have deemed it expedient to arrange these illusions under three different heads, viz.—

1. The illusion of Happy Phrases.
2. The illusion of the Grand Tour.
3. The illusion of the *Doctrinaire.*

But before entering on this part of my task I wish to say that in the remarks I am about to make on the Press, I allude exclusively to the great London 'Dailies,' as being the Papers with which I am best acquainted, and in these only to the political *editorials*—all the other parts, which are under the direct charge of men of special knowledge and ability in the various departments of literature, art, music, the drama, trade, and the like, being on the whole excellent.

(1) And first as to the *Illusion of Happy Phrases.* These 'happy phrases,' as they are

called by the Press (and which now appear to be the main foundation on which political reputations rest), consist in certain light and more or less flippant epigrams, such as 'mending and ending,' 'plundering and blundering,' 'rescue and retire,' and the like, which by their piquancy or picturesqueness strike the fancy and abide in the memory, but which like puns are in themselves mere literary exercises, mere exaggerations, which like artificial crystals can only get their appearance of regularity and finish by the process of trimming down, filling out, or in other ways rounding off the rough edges and corners of truth; and in the complex web of facts involved in practical politics serve rather to perplex and obscure than to instruct the judgment. They are, as I have said, mere *literary* exercises, and afford therefore as little evidence of qualification for the high duties of the Statesman and practical politician, as they do for those of the engineer, the soldier, the surgeon, or the shoemaker. They are admissible, it is true, in the barrister, as his business is to do his best by word-glamour and sophistry to make the worse appear the better reason; but then he is perfectly harmless, for you have a judge above him to reduce his high-flown and vaporous epigrams to their true proportions. But in Parliament and Politics where you have no high and judicial authority to intervene, where the People are at the mercy of the phrase-monger, and the Press shares the illusion of the People, these 'happy phrases,' to which the Press attaches so much importance, become positively noxious, and are a source indirectly of real public danger. Now all greatness whatever, it will be generally admitted, whether it be of the Thinker, the Poet, the Mathematician, the General, the Physician, or the Chess-player, consists in the perception of wider, more varied, more subtle, or more complex relations between the *real facts* or things with which it deals; and the same is true of Statesmanship. But so little evidently has this facility in producing epigrams, puns, or other 'happy phrases' that depend on *literary exaggeration* or distortion, to do with it, that, as we should expect beforehand, the two qualities or kinds of ability are very rarely found united in the same person. Instead therefore of the Press taking it for granted (or allowing it to be taken for granted) that the one kind of ability affords a presumption of the other, it ought rather to start with the assumption (unless on special and rigorous proof shown) that the possession of the one renders the presence of the other unlikely. For after all, what is this illusion of 'happy phrases' but another form of the same illusion which we saw was so common among men when gathered in masses, the illusion, viz. of taking the Talker for the Thinker, the man who gives expression to a common want or sentiment, for the man who is fitted by nature or study to see its worth, weigh its wisdom, or devise means for carrying it into practical effect; the only difference being that whereas the People in general will (as we saw in the case of Lord Randolph Churchill) swallow the 'happy phrase' in its most crude, virulent, and undigested state, the Editor in his study prefers it, if it can be had, in a more refined, polished, and literary form. But if, as we have seen in a previous chapter, the qualities essential to the Statesman are as different and distinct in nature from those of the 'happy phrase-monger' as the qualities of the skilled physician are from those of the quack; and if the object of all political effort is to find the man most capable of grasping the central truths on which the complex facts of political affairs turn; it is evident that the political guides who confound them, instead of guarding us from the Demagogue, must be mainly responsible for thrusting him upon us. And that this is indeed what the Press has done, and is doing, I shall now endeavour to prove.

I take up, for example, a random copy of the *Pall Mall Gazette*, which happens to be lying beside me on the day on which I am making notes. for this and the preceding chapter, and on looking through it come on some comments of the Editor on a speech of Lord Salisbury's, then recently delivered, which may serve to illustrate my meaning. The Editor, after remarking that the speech was full of happy phrases, mentions the following remarks as great hits,— (1) "Progress has different definitions in different countries, and in this country it means taking something from the landlords;" (2) "Confidence is frequently a short and easy course to the Bankruptcy Court;" (3) "Coercion is nothing more than forcing people to abstain from a peculiar mode of propagating their political opinions," and admiringly asserts that these happy phrases are just the sort of thing to make a reputation in the House of Commons, that is to say, to pave the way to a seat in the Cabinet and on to the Premiership itself. Now the most cursory examination of these specimens of 'happy phrases' will show that the first is not true, and can only get what pregnancy it has by stretching the truth to that point of exaggeration where it becomes a falsehood; the second is a pure platitude *à la* Martin Tupper; and the last, in the sense in which it is applied to the Irish people, is a mere stilted form of expression, nothing more. The reader will therefore judge whether such purely literary trifling should be any better passport to success in Parliament and a seat in the Cabinet, and in consequence to the making or mending of laws, than to a seat on a bench of physicians or cobblers, and the curing of bodies or mending of shoes; and whether it constitutes any higher qualification for the management of the business of a nation, than it would for the management of a private business like that of Mr. Shoolbred or Mr. Whiteley. And yet this stuff, which could, I will venture to say, be turned out by the ream by the worst paid hack on his own journal, is the sort of thing the Editor admiringly admits is fitted to make a reputation in the House of Commons! The same journal, commenting a short time afterwards on a speech of Mr. Sexton's in reply to one of Mr. Chamberlain on the Irish Home Rule Bill, selects the following passages from the speech as 'a series of extremely brilliant thrusts,' with the remark that at the end of the speech, "the House roared with laughter and rang with cheers, and Mr. Sexton had placed his claim to rank among the three best debaters in the House beyond a doubt." Here are the 'extremely brilliant thrusts' referred to :—(1) "Powerful as a coadjutor, impotent as a rebel;" (2) "Speaking with a sepulchral voice like one which comes from a cave;" (3) "The ally of Tories, the confederate of Whigs, the deserter of his own party;" (4) "The nature and intent of the Right Hon. Gentleman is to be a mayor." Now it is apparent that all this is a mere exercise of literary ingenuity, differing in no other respect from the stuffed-club style of Lord Randolph Churchill than in having a more refined literary edge; and bringing us no nearer the solution of the Irish or any other problem than the problem of the moon. For, as before, the most casual examination will show that the first of these 'extremely brilliant thrusts' is a mere exaggeration, so manipulated (to get the antithesis) as to become untrue; the second is a mere play on words; the third a piece of high-sounding rhetoric only; and the last a purely personal impertinence. The above are only a few examples picked up at the time, but the point of view of the paper is still essentially the same. The reader will therefore judge for himself whether an Editor who of all others pretends to lead the van and to believe that 'government by journalism' has now come, yet who is so lost in admiration of this kind of trifling, and so sunk in the illusion that adroitness and facility in turning out this mere literary and rhetorical jingle, establishes a man's rank as a debater and statesman, is more likely to precipitate the phrase-monger and demagogue upon us, or to defend us from him.

Take again the *Daily News*, the organ of the Liberal Party, and a high-class journal of unimpeachable respectability and wide political influence. Some time about the beginning of the present year '86, a remarkable change was observable in the tone of the leading articles in this paper towards the personality and performance of Lord Randolph Churchill. Hitherto it had regarded him (according to Lord Randolph Churchill himself) as an 'incompetent idiot,' and a 'most abandoned and unscrupulous politician,' when lo! all of a sudden a leading article appeared in which he was described, intellectually at least, in terms of the highest eulogy and admiration. Surprised at this unexpected change of tone, on making inquiries I ascertained that there had been a change in the editorship of the paper, and that the new Editor was none other than the Editor of Lord Randolph Churchill's own speeches, in the introduction to which I had already observed what appeared to me some most curious and unaccountable political and literary judgments. On further inquiry I learned also that he was the author of a work entitled *A Diary of two Parliaments*, and being curious to know what the literary standpoint could be from which such singular judgments had proceeded, I at once turned to the volume, and had not read many pages before my curiosity at what had previously puzzled me was fully set at rest. "Here," I said to myself as I read along, "you have the admirer of 'happy phrases' in his highest state of ecstasy;" and as I observed the way in which he bent before the coiners of these phrases, and the tortures to which he himself put the English language in his efforts to emulate them, I felt that if imitation is the sincerest flattery, there could be no doubt of the depth and sincerity of his admiration. As regards the matter of the book, I have no call at present to speak. I may only say in passing, that it is precisely what you might have expected from one who had been condemned to sit for years as a reporter in the gallery of the House of Commons. A mere chronicle of the remarks made by honourable members to one another and to the House, of their appearance and movements, but especially of their changes of costume, 'of their cuts and condescensions,' of how this noble lord was seen talking to that hon. member, and the like;—and all with the pomp and gusto with which the footman might recount the conversation of his master's guests in the servants' hall; the entrance of some of the poorer Irish members into the House being regarded with that horror and supercilious disgust with which one of these well-fed lacqueys regards the presence of the 'poor relation' in the drawing-room. But it is in his style and manner, as I have said, that you see the man and his admirations, and the secret of his literary and political judgments. Of this style and manner I can give the reader no better general impression than by remarking that they bear the same relation to ordinary English that the Christy minstrel version of the song of 'Old Uncle Ned' bears to the original version. The original has it that old Uncle Ned who lived a long time ago "had no hair on the top of his head, just the place where the hair ought to grow." In the Christy minstrel version it runs that "he had no capillary substance on the summit of his pericranium, just the position where the said capillary substance ought to vegetate." Now this is precisely the style and key in which the *Diary of Two Parliaments* is written throughout, but lest this may seem an exaggeration, I may be permitted to give a few quotations picked out here and there at random. One hon. member's handkerchief becomes in the author's description, "this particular article of portable property;" the snuff-box of another is "not an article that would lie in the waistcoat-pocket, but a roomy box such as might on occasion serve to carry the necessaries of a night's journey, or peradventure to accommodate itself as a portable bath;" while the hon. member who sat on the bench immediately beneath it is described as having " moved away lest he should be crushed in its ruins as it fell"! General Burnaby made a short speech of " five sentences long," which is characterized as " a jewel worthy to sparkle for all ages on the outstretched forefinger of Time"! The Whigs are described as "those uncertain compounds of slow-moving impulse, *entrées* in the feast of politics." Of Lord Spencer and his brother it is remarked, that " by the grave face of the Earl who knows so much about Ireland are displayed the dazzling glories of the laundress which shed a starchy halo around the form of his young brother"! Twice in four pages tailoring is described as the 'sartorial art.' On a rose in Mr. Gladstone's coat we have the following remark,—" The only truculent thing anywhere about was the great red rose in the Premier's coat with its leaves all awry, as if it had already been in battle;" and on a new coat worn by him, " The Premier had relinquished a tenant's interest in a familiar garment, and had entered upon a fresh holding, where (as is provided for in the fourth clause of the Land Bill) he found the incidence of tenancy subject to incommodious statutory conditions!"

Such is the Editor of the *Daily News*, and the reader will now have little difficulty in understanding the sudden change that came over the paper with regard to the ability and performance of Lord Randolph Churchill, and will realize that its Editor would naturally see in such kindred examples of his style as I have quoted in a former chapter, strokes of real genius, and in his career one which "for brilliancy it would be difficult to parallel." The reader will also judge whether one who is so great an admirer of 'happy phrases,' and who in his own most ambitious efforts to imitate them can rise no higher than the Christy-minstrel version of 'Old Uncle Ned,' is an intellectual instrument fit to instruct the Public in its choice of wise statesmen, or is likely soon to purge the Phrase-monger and Demagogue away.

Take again the *Times* and the *Standard*. Of the Editor of the *Standard* I am unable to judge from his articles to what extent he is himself personally under the illusion of 'happy phrases'; but I can only remark, that if he was sincere in his judgment of Lord Randolph Churchill (and I am obliged to take Lord Randolph Churchill as my text, as being in style, ability, and general pose the only example of the pure demagogue at present in the front ranks of English politics), when about a year ago, after contemplating his whole career, he said that he had shown no more political knowledge fitting him for his high position than an overgrown schoolboy, it is simply incredible that he can be sincere *now*,* when he preaches the opposite view, and bows to that public opinion which by advertisement he has helped to create; and if he had the insight to see through his poor tricks *then*, but (failing to bring the party over to his views) now shuts his eyes, winks hard, and applauds with the multitude; the result is the same as if he were himself personally under this illusion of 'happy phrases.' In either case he is useless in helping us to keep out the Demagogue, or in assisting us in the choice of wise and good leaders.

Of the *Times* itself little need here be said. I have already shown how relentlessly in the old days of its undisputed supremacy it drew the

* Autumn '86.

line between the Phrase-monger and the Statesman; and I still can perceive in its leaders that the traditions of its prime, although too often ignored, are not altogether forgotten. But having become a mere Party journal, it is obliged to respect the feelings of its *clientèle*, and uses its better insight rather for the aggrandizement of its own party than for the public good. Instead of applying its gauge rigorously to friend and foe alike, it now applies it arbitrarily; so that while rarely failing to point out that any specially telling personality in the speech of its political opponents is not 'statesmanship,' it quite overlooks this distinction in similar remarks of its political friends. And accordingly in almost every issue while the House is sitting, you will find its editorials all cunningly constructed on this one plan. If, for example, the phrase-monger who makes the 'happy hit' is on its own side in politics, the editorial comment will run somewhat in this way—" The vigorous and pungent strictures of the hon. member fell with telling force on the House," &c.; if on the opposite side, the hon. member will have " surpassed himself in audacious quibbling with plain issues, in juggling with empty phrases, and in perverting notorious facts," or the like. If, on the contrary, the speech of its opponent is dull, the hon. member will have "bored the House with his dreary platitudes until its patience was exhausted," &c.; while the dulness of its friend's speech will be treated in this way—" We have no attempt here at windy rhetoric, no turning aside to substitute the pitiful dexterities of personal dialectics for a business-like examination of the issue before the House." And so on throughout. It is evident therefore that the *Times*, like the *Standard*, although not so hopelessly sunk in the illusion of 'happy phrases' as some other leading journals, is impotent to defend us from the Phrase-monger and Demagogue whom it once so much dreaded, by reason of its having now become a mere Party organ, and thus having placed its great powers at the service of a class rather than of the State.

I have selected the four journals above mentioned as being those with which I am personally most familiar, and whose tone and point of view I have most carefully watched, and also as being fairly typical of the best London journalism; the other papers, so far as I have read them, differing from these in no essential respect either in their tone or point of view. And now before passing on it may be interesting to inquire how this excessive reverence for 'happy phrases,' this tendency to mingle and confound the Phrase-monger and Statesman, has originated. For my own part I believe it to be largely due to the combined influence exerted over the Press as a body by the great names of Macaulay and Lord Beaconsfield. Many of the leader writers on the great 'Dailies,' who are at once literary men and politicians, have consciously adopted Macaulay as their model of literary style; and all of them, I presume, have been deeply impressed with the success of Lord Beaconsfield's political career. And as both Macaulay and Lord Beaconsfield (who were themselves at once literary men and politicians) rose into power in the first instance by the same means—Macaulay by his 'epigrammatic style,' Beaconsfield by his 'happy phrases,' —it is evident that unless great discrimination were exercised, there would be a tendency to confound 'phrasemongering' in general with 'statesmanship,' and to augur a like success to the aspiring imitators as had attended the careers of their illustrious prototypes. For although it is now generally admitted that it was by over-straining his epigrams to the point at which they did violence to the truth, that Macaulay succeeded in getting some of his most brilliant effects, nevertheless his name with the Press is still a potent one to conjure with. And although Beaconsfield's rise into power by means of his 'happy phrases' occurred at a time when no great domestic problems connected with land or capital had yet arisen to divide and exasperate classes, when a government still aristocratic gave strength and directness to foreign policy, and the *Times* sat high over all guarding the interests of the State (and when the country in consequence would have run little risk even if the Whigs and Tories had selected their respective champions from the men who could stand longest on their heads); still when a man rises to be Prime Minister by *any* means, I for one should despair of proving to the great masses of men that these means were poor and unworthy. And yet to tolerate that at the present time when circumstances have entirely changed, when foreign policy is almost literally at the mercy of the distracted multitude, and when the war between landlord and tenant, capital and labour is about to begin, a man should rise by mere 'happy phrases' to positions of political power, can only be possible to those who are so wrapped up in hearsays and great names that they will not take the trouble to lift the veil that enshrouds them and shear the illusions away. And it is in my opinion precisely because the Press has not taken the pains to do this, that you have it still holding on to the shadowy weapons associated with the names of these great men (at a time too when circumstances have entirely changed, and weapons other than mere literary phrases are necessary to meet them); still pushing into public notice and awarding the palm of honour without suspicion or hesitation to all manner of word-mongers, virulent or refined; the consequence being, that aspirants for Parliamentary position (taking advantage of this weakness of the Press) instead of applying themselves to the great principles of government, and storing their minds with great masses of orderly and digested detail, are to be seen competing with one another in the privacy of their studies in the manufacture of 'happy phrases,' which, intended at first for some local audience perhaps, are really constructed with an eye to their effect on the Press—which will report them, appraise them, circulate them, and give them currency with the masses. And hence it is that you have political reputations almost literally made in the first place, and afterwards sustained, by such phrases as 'Mending and ending,' 'Whigs bathing,' 'Rescue and retire,' 'Extinct volcanoes,' 'Peace with honour,' 'Plundering and blundering,' 'The policy of scuttle,' 'Leaps and bounds,' and the like; even a man of the intellectual calibre of Mr. John Morley being obliged to play down to this poor illusion;—and all this too (greatest satire of all) when you can find as much of this stuff and of as good a quality in a week in *Punch* and the other comic and satirical journals as would supply the whole House for a session; the professional authors differing from the amateurs only in this, that instead of looking forward to a seat in the Cabinet, or to the Premiership itself as the result of their efforts, like other caterers for the Public they are only too happy if they can make sure of punctual pay and steady employment.

(2) If, as we have seen, some of the London 'Dailies,' although practically bending to the illusion of 'happy phrases,' are less immersed in it than others; all alike may be said to be submerged in the second illusion which I have mentioned

above, viz. the *Illusion of the 'Grand Tour.'* And perhaps I cannot better explain what I mean by this than by saying that if you take three or four of the younger leaders of either of the great Parliamentary parties (all about equal in position and popularity), and start any one of them in a period of political expectancy on a starring expedition through the country, making the 'grand tour' around by Edinburgh, Glasgow, and the North; you will find that although in his progress he has only given expression to the ordinary recognized and long understood policy of the Party, the din and uproar caused by the political and party bagpipes in the Press will have so stamped his name on the public imagination, that on his return the old equality of political rank between him and his comrades will have undergone a complete and entire metamorphosis; the same change and evolution having taken place among them as is seen when an ordinary bee is, by the greater attention paid to it, fattened into a queen bee; the mere echo and reverberation of his name throughout the length and breadth of the land (for no number of isolated, casual, or irregular speeches inadequately reported can compare in effect with the concentration of the whole Press on a single speech, or series of speeches) having so heightened his reputation, and filled the public ear, that his former equals, by a kind of public and informal *plébiscite*, will have quietly and unconsciously sunk the while into an inferior and subordinate position. I happened, for example, to be in Scotland in the autumn of '85, when Mr. Chamberlain started on his grand tour through the North; and in the absence of any other star of the first magnitude on the political horizon he so concentrated on himself for a week or two the gaze and attention of the Public, that although at starting he was confessedly only one among a number of prominent Radicals all about his equals in political rank and repute, by the time he returned (although he had only been the mouthpiece for the time being of what government members of the party had long been advocating in the magazines and journals, in Parliament and out of it) he was dilated to so portentous a bulk that from that day onwards his comrades, in presence of the surge of admiration that swelled around him, could only sink back and hide for the time their diminished heads in the crowd. So great indeed was his success, that in the temporary silence and retirement of Mr. Gladstone he so overshadowed for the moment his old leader, that the latter had to be heralded back into the field again with the sound of trumpets, and there put forth the whole strength of his great name and prestige to regain his former authority; almost endangering the unity of the party before he succeeded in superseding the 'unauthorized programme' of his ambitious subordinate by a programme of his own. The same change in relative positions occurred when Mr. John Morley, owing to his Home Rule predilections, was made Irish secretary; and so shared with Mr. Gladstone the attention of the world. Mr. Chamberlain having accepted a less prominent situation in the Cabinet, and being for the moment left in the political shade, the Press immediately fell into its old illusion, remarking that "Mr. Morley had improved his position in the party at the expense of Mr. Chamberlain;"— poor Mr. Trevelyan, in the meantime, who had refused office in the Government, and who for some length of time had kept in the political background, being out of the running altogether. Indeed it was not until the opposition to the Home Rule Bill became acute under the leadership of Lord Hartington and Mr. Chamberlain, that the latter, by the interest which was again concentrated on him by the Press, succeeded in making himself once more an object of interest and attention. Even as I write,* the same effect of the grand tour may be seen going on before our very eyes. Lord Salisbury, at a time when the whole country is eagerly waiting for some intimation of the new Tory Programme, instead of coming forward in person to announce the policy of the Government (holding all his subordinates in the leash the while), consents (fatal error) to allow Lord Randolph Churchill to go to Dartford and Bradford as its exponent and spokesman. The result has been what indeed might have been foreseen; the whole Press at once, and with one accord, seize on the circumstance as another proof that Lord Randolph Churchill is the real leader of the Party, and treat him as such; whereas had Lord Salisbury come forward with his policy in person, the Press, however much they might have suspected that Lord Randolph Churchill had secretly initiated it, would have felt and announced that Lord Salisbury was

* Autumn '86.

still the strong man in the Cabinet; and he would thus have immensely strengthened a position which by this false step has for the time being been seriously weakened. It was said to be the secret of Buonaparte's military success that he exhausted all his ingenuity in manœuvring to bring his battalions at such an angle to the enemy that against each of their men he should be able to confront two of his own. It is the secret of Parliamentary success, to manœuvre so as to get yourself at that angle where the Press shall be obliged to mention your name twice to your opponent's or competitor's once. This, in a word, is the meaning of that illusion of the 'Grand Tour' in which the Press is immersed; and by taking advantage of which you may almost undertake to predict that by judicious management and handling, out of an ordinary working member of Parliament a Cabinet Minister may be made in six months, with the possible reversion to the Premiership in twelve! Is this not pitiful? That the People should imagine that they hear the voice of a god in one with whose name the whole land is ringing, and that with them a man's reputation should rise or fall according to the number of times his name is mentioned in a penny newspaper, is (in the absence of any other means of knowing) natural enough; but that the Press, whose office it is to be the zealous guardian of the State, and to smelt away the dross from the gold in political reputations, should be brow-beaten and subdued by this shallow artifice, proves how far towards the reign of the Demagogue we have already arrived.

(3) If the two illusions of the Press which I have just illustrated—the illusion of 'happy phrases' and the illusion of the 'grand tour'—have a *direct* tendency to thrust on us the Demagogue instead of defending us from him, this tendency is *indirectly* furthered by a third illusion and prejudice under which the Press labours; and by which the natural enemies of the Demagogue and Phrase-coiner—viz. the men of Thought—are prevented from exercising their normal and legitimate influence over the People. This illusion and prejudice, which operate in much the same way as a prejudice against cats might do when it was a question of the extermination of rats, I have called the *Illusion of the 'Doctrinaire.'*

In the old days, when the country was governed by the great Territorial Houses; and men of wealth and material standing were alone possessed of the franchise; literary men of all kinds—philosophers, publicists, political thinkers, historians, and the like—were not encouraged by the ruling powers to interfere in politics; and the *Times*, which directly represented the feelings, interests, and prejudices of these privileged classes, would sooner, as has often been said, have seen the country elect an alderman or fox-hunter than any political thinker however eminent or profound. But while thus jealously repudiating the Political Thinker, the ruling families of both Parties were always glad to secure any facile phrase-monger, literary fencer, or the like (who had by accident or good fortune succeeded in getting into the House), to lead the debates; and were always ready and willing to give him, if successful in fighting their battles and carrying out their wishes, substantial recognition, promotion, and advancement; as was the case with Burke, Canning, Disraeli, Gladstone, and the rest. But although in a Parliamentary Government where legislation goes by public speaking, the Phrase-monger and *literateur* must always occupy an important place, the ruling powers did not wish it so to appear to the world; for had once the idea got abroad that 'literary men' were the natural leaders of the respective parties; and that (when once accredited) they would tend more and more as Democracy approached to initiate and direct policy as well as to expound and defend it; all Grub Street, swollen into importance, would have risen in mutiny at its exclusion from political influence; and the Aristocracy would in a great measure have lost their political prestige and authority—a result which no class of men accustomed to power could be expected patiently to abide. Accordingly a set of phrases had to be invented which would instil the necessary distinction into the public mind; and keep all sweet, smooth, and tranquil as before. The *Times* accordingly, as the literary agent of the ruling classes, undertook the problem; and succeeded in striking out the necessary distinctions with entire and happy success. For from thenceforth, through its promulgation, it became established that the literary leaders of the respective parties *inside* the House (who had been recruited, as I have said, from the literary class, for their power of coining 'happy phrases,' and whose style and methods were still as literary as in their days of obscurity) should be dignified by the title of 'Statesmen'; while the whole body and tribe of them *outside* the House or Cabinet—publicists, *literateurs,* thinkers, political historians, and all —were mere 'viewy literary politicians,' mere '*doctrinaires,*' and the like. No sooner was this distinction announced and spread abroad by the *Times,* than all those who were possessed of the franchise—the manufacturers, merchants, shopkeepers, and financiers, in a word, all the monied classes in the kingdom who had been nurtured in aristocratic traditions of Government —accepted it with delight as a kind of ordinance of nature. For although it is as certain as that a stone when thrown into the air will fall to the ground, that in Parliamentary Government by Party and Debate, the literary fencer will lead; and that (unless sternly suppressed by the Press) to him and his like the best offices will fall; still it would be too much for human nature to allow that men whom they had regarded from afar off as a herd of scribblers (many of them out-at-elbows) should have the control of that high imperial policy which had hitherto been the prerogative of the Aristocracy alone. And accordingly from this time onwards, the flimsy and baseless distinction between the 'Statesman' and the '*Doctrinaire*' (according as they were *within* or *without* the enchanted circle of the Cabinet) became embodied as an article of belief in English politics, where it remains to this day.

Now all this was natural enough at a time when the Aristocracy was the ruling power in the State; when the franchise was limited to a select and monied class brought up in traditions of aristocratic prestige and predominance; and when the *Times* as their literary agent and representative upheld the solid political and material interests of both. What I find fault with is, that now that the Aristocracy is no longer the ruling power in the State; that by the extension of the suffrage Democracy is practically here, and the arena in consequence is open to talent; now that all the currents both of public opinion and the Press have set towards the apotheosis of the happy Phrase-monger and the Demagogue; men of political thought and culture (who are the natural enemies of these and the best make-weights against them) should be boycotted and handicapped by this old, absurd, and empty illusion, indoctrinated in other days, by other men, and for other purposes. That this is so there can be little doubt. When John Morley, for example (a typical instance of the deep and cultured political thinker), had made his way into the Cabinet independently of the Press, both Lord Salisbury and Lord Randolph Churchill (God save the mark!) took the opportunity of referring to the appointment in public; and while admitting his eminence in literature, questioned whether a mere 'literary man' was fit to administer the affairs of a great country; and in both instances, I observed, the remark was not only received with applause by the respective audiences (as was natural from the ideas with which they had been indoctrinated), but was acquiesced in, as far as common decency would permit, by a large section of the Press. So deeply indeed had both the Public and the Press been imbued with this old illusion of the *Times*, that it never seems to have occurred to them that both Lord Salisbury and Lord Randolph Churchill had themselves made their way into the Cabinet because they were 'literary men': the former, because of his power of caustic epigram which pleased the cultivated, and was a relic of the time when he was a Saturday Reviewer; the latter, because he was a literary 'bruiser' and lampooner who had pleased the mob! And yet after all this objection and hesitation shown to Mr. Morley before and at the time of his entering the Cabinet, he had only to be in it a month or two when, hey, presto! he is suddenly transformed from the '*doctrinaire*' to the 'statesman' (as if his mode of argument and debate after entering the Cabinet could have differed in any respect from that adopted while he was outside it); all the other political thinkers meanwhile who were still without the fold, having the door shut in the face of their advancement (by reason of the prejudice excited against them as '*doctrinaires*') until they shall be able to make their way into it either by turning their wits to epigram making, political lampooning, or some other species of phrase-mongering, or by taking the 'stump' and going the round of the country on the 'grand tour.' Even the *Times* itself, which was, and still is, the main repository of this illusion and prejudice; and which still professes to over-rule the decisions of Cabinets;—what is its editor but a '*doctrinaire*'? and what are the political arguments by which it advocates or rejects any course of policy but (by its own definition) the arguments of a *doctrinaire?* So that as effect and upshot of this really poor illusion we have this curious result, that if a man belongs to the *lower* or lowest type of literary man, if he is a maker of epigrams, a punster, or even a literary lampooner like Lord Randolph Churchill (and so is either useful in the House as a party skirmisher, or out of it pleases the *dilettante* by his epigrams, or the mob by his violence of language), he can be almost assured of attaining a seat in the Cabinet and councils of State, and so becoming a 'Statesman'; while, on the contrary, if he is the *high* type of literary man—the wide and cultured political thinker like Mr. Stuart Mill or Mr. Morley—he can barely attain a seat in the House (let alone in the Cabinet), because of the prejudice excited against him by the Press! But the absurdity reaches its climax when we consider that it is not even of the best literary men in their own line that Cabinet Ministers and Premiers are made, but only of such a scratch assortment as by other means—wealth, position, local influence, and the like—have succeeded in making their way into the House. For I will undertake to find in a single article of the *Saturday Review* more epigrammatic power than in a dozen speeches of Lord Salisbury; more real humour, fun, and effective political caricature in a single number of *Punch* than in half-a-dozen nights' debates; and more real insight into political facts and their relations, connections, and meanings in a single copy of the *Spectator*, than in all the collected speeches by which Lord Randolph Churchill rose to power. And yet if the one set of men appeared on a political platform to solicit the suffrages of their fellow subjects, the fact of their being *littérateurs*, even political *littérateurs*, would detract from, rather than add to, their chances of success as being ' doctrinaires'; while the others would, as 'statesmen,' strike the stars with their sublime heads. And with what further result? Why this,—that men whose shoe-latchets Cabinet Ministers, in that very line by which they rose to power, would be unworthy to unloose, are obliged in the great problems of society and the world to subordinate their own special and peculiar genius; and to become to these, ministers, train-bearers, and satellites merely. Here, for example, is Lord Randolph Churchill, whose spoken or written thoughts or style never rise above the level of the most ordinary country newspaper; who, I will venture to say, could no more write a connected treatise on Politics, Political Economy, Political History, or the like, that first-rate literary men would recognize and pass, than build the pyramids; yet when he brings his poor stock-in-trade of literary ware—his 'immense deliberation,' 'tremendous liabilities,' 'prodigious imbecility,' 'sinister machinations,' &c.—to the House of Commons; and firing them off recklessly at friend and foe alike, has them blown around the world by the Press; he soon comes to bestride the political world; and literary men of great reach and ability are forced to walk between his legs and find themselves what independent foothold and leverage they may. But this illusion, bred and propagated by the literary men of the Press themselves, is sadly avenged on them. For to be condemned to go through this life studying and discussing (as if they were serious political achievements) such mere paltry literary phrases as 'the policy of scuttle,' 'Whigs bathing,' 'rescue and retire,' 'extinct volcanoes,' and the like—I never think of it without being reminded of those priests of the Grand Lama of Thibet, who regarded his very excrement as of so sacred and sovereign a nature, that they reverently collected it, and with their own hands patiently worked it up into dough pills for the cure and salvation of the world. And thus the tendency to choose the Demagogue which arises from the illusion of 'happy phrases' and of the 'grand tour' with which the press is imbued, is aggravated by the further prejudice excited against men of real thought and culture by this illusion of the '*doctrinaire.*' Under these circumstances the reader will judge whether, with its manifold mops, the Press is likely to succeed in keeping out the evils that come with the advancing sweep of Democracy, or the Demagogue that rides on the crest of its wave.

Such then are the three great intellectual illusions under which the Press labours at the present time—the illusion of 'happy phrases,' of the 'grand tour,' and of the '*doctrinaire*,'—each of which has a tendency to precipitate on us the Demagogue rather than to defend us from him.

Now if the conclusions arrived at in the present and preceding chapters be true, and if I have been guilty of no exaggeration of fact (for some exaggeration of phrase perhaps was inevitable to emphasize my meaning), they should hold good in the future as well as in the present and past; and so be capable of being brought to a definite and practical test. And as I believe that the relations of the Press to Politics and the Public are likely to remain pretty much the same as they are now through the whole of what may be called the Newspaper Era; and as, furthermore, I consider that no speculative Thinker is, vulgarly speaking, 'worth his salt' unless his opinions lie so close to the central and moving tendencies by which society is impelled, that they will in their general scope and direction bear the strain of prediction,—to this test I am accordingly willing to submit them. And hence I am prepared to affirm :—

(1) That in all large popular and representative bodies, where Government is carried on by Debate and by the rotation of Parties, there must at all times and places be a tendency for the Demagogue or Phrase-monger, unless specially guarded against, to rise to power.

(2) That in the Newspaper Era of democracies, when the Press (as at present among ourselves) is from circumstances obliged to renounce its high and proper function as the impartial *judge* and *winnower* of reputations, and to become a

mere organ for focussing, concentrating, and in the end echoing and *reflecting* the public opinion of the different *parties* in the State; when (with Demos sitting as judge) it follows pen in hand the track of rival political orators and epigrammatists, reporting their public and parliamentary speeches at full length for the breakfast-table, and (itself under the illusion of 'happy phrases,' or forced to appear so) picks out their epigrams as particular plums in the banquet, setting them flying around the world to be read of all; you can predict with as much certainty that the Phrase-monger and Demagogue will become triumphant in Politics, and that to the best performer in these lines the best places in the government will fall (provided all start even), as you can that the like success will attend his brother of the theatre or Music-Hall; while political thinkers of insight and culture (who are the natural enemies of the Phrase-monger and Demagogue) are kept out of power by the prejudice excited against them as '*doctrinaires*' by the Press.

(3) That if, on the other hand, one of a number of political aspirants of equal promise should by chance or circumstance get the start of the rest, and by being first in the field (doing the

'grand tour,' and making himself for the time being the mouthpiece of the party) so concentrate on himself the attention of the entire Press day by day as to make his name a household word; you will then have as leader, a hap-hazard leader,—a man of real ability or of none, as the case may be,—and political reputations will be seen to rise or fall in relation to each other largely in proportion to the *prominence* with which respective politicians keep themselves before the public eye.

(4) That, owing to the relation of the Press to Party Politics, and the pressure thus put upon it, individual newspapers sitting in *political* judgment will be obliged to see brilliancy and wit in the efforts of the men thus thrust into positions of importance, which, were they sitting in *literary* judgment, they would pass by with contempt and reprobation; and will be obliged to find in political platitudes such as may be any night heard at a boys' debating school, masterpieces of statesmanship and genius.

(5) And worse than all, that, as we saw in the case of Lord Randolph Churchill, the Press (having to *reflect* and echo, and not to *direct* the opinion of the party and the hour) while not denying that a course of unscrupulous

conduct, which on any theory of reward and punishment should have consigned its author to political damnation, has really been the means of his political apotheosis; assents to it not only without reprobation, but (as one sees between the lines) with a kind of secret admiration; thus indirectly encouraging all ambitious men to reach at political power by these or the like unworthy means; and so rendering it probable, nay certain, that in future (and indeed so long as the present relation of the Press to Parliament and the Public lasts) to the vices of the political Phrase-monger and Demagogue to which the Press must lead us, you will have to add the vices of what Mr. Goldwin Smith calls the 'political scoundrel.'

And now I have done. I have traced in a general way the career of Lord Randolph Churchill from the time of his emergence on the political horizon, to the time of his accession to power. I have described the vicissitudes of his rise, the impressions made by his performance on the House, the Press, the Public, and his own Party, at the various stages of his career; and the way in which these various elements of opinion acted and reacted on each other (each heightening and intensifying the rest), until his reputation, which started on an admitted basis of levity and unscrupulousness, grew (by the mere echo and reverberation of itself in the Press as he went along) in bulk and importance, like a snowball, rather by the accumulation of the same than by the incorporation of new and higher elements, until, filling the political horizon, and tinged by imagination, it stood out against the sky transformed into a colossal image of political power and greatness. I next, in order to discover the real basis of power and ability on which so huge a superstructure had been reared, submitted his political performances to analysis; and found that as regards his Oratory (which I had good opportunity of comparing with both great and ordinary models) it would with its slow, harsh, and leaden delivery, unrelieved by any gleams of genial humour, brilliancy, or wit, and grinding along in a sullen monotony of vituperation and abuse, instead of entitling him to become a Minister of the Crown, have given him not even a third-rate position at Cogers' Hall; and that as regards his Statesmanship, nowhere in the long line of speeches by which he rose to power, and through which I had to wade, did one single political principle, observation, or reflection emerge which could with fairness be regarded as above the level of the most ordinary and current platitude; that instead of the grasp and comprehension of the Statesman, you had the arts of the Demagogue flourishing in all their luxuriance throughout—arts which I then proceeded to illustrate at full length, and in abundance of detail. But knowing well that the dazzling radiance of his success would not only palliate and gild the deep reprobation of his rise, but would (in spite of all I could say) be held as symbol and guarantee of a wide sea of hidden and unfathomable power yet to be revealed; and perceiving as I did that his rise was due, not to any particular ability or virtue in himself, but to defects in the institutions which permitted and even aided it; I felt that my demonstration would have little effect, unless I could put my finger on those flaws and spots in our political system which permitted so great a success to erect itself on so slender a stock of ability; and so show that his rise, instead of being unnatural, was, when well seen, precisely what under favourable circumstances you could have predicted, and can predict again. With this object in view I then entered on an examination of our present democratic institutions,—their dangers, their tendencies, their safeguards, and the like,—and at last came to the breach in that ring-fence which hedges the approaches to power through which not only he had entered in, but through which his successors may still follow. I showed that the only institution which had the power and prestige necessary to keep out the Demagogue—viz. the Newspaper Press—was the one which, instead of shutting him out, freely invited him in; and on inquiring finally how this curious result arose, I found it due in the first place to the almost inevitable relation at present existing between the Press on the one hand, and Parliament and the Public on the other; in the second place, to certain great intellectual illusions with which the Press is imbued—illusions which have a direct tendency to precipitate the Demagogue on us, and not to defend us from him. In this way I have endeavoured to make it apparent that the success of Lord Randolph Churchill on the poor stock of ability with which I have credited him, is not a miracle, but is a necessary result of political conditions existing at the present time; and that under favouring circumstances a like success could be predicted again to-morrow.

And now in conclusion I desire to say, that feeling as I do that in the rise of Lord Randolph Churchill a greater blow than any in my time has been struck not only at those high intellectual requisites for Statesmanship which we expect in the rulers of a great Empire, but at political morality itself; as well as at all those great ideals of thought, conduct, and action which men hold most dear; and feeling also that the fact that so great a success could be reared on such ability and conduct has already let down the tone of political honour to a depth from which it will not again easily emerge (for who, with this splendid example before him, will hesitate to misrepresent, to exaggerate, to lampoon, to caricature, and to abuse, when such a course, if not openly applauded, yet secretly favours rather than retards, both with the Press and the Public, the chances of that very success which with the majority of mankind is itself the sign of greatness); I determined that no effort of mine, however inadequate, should be spared to direct the attention of the Public, and especially of all leaders of opinion, to the subject; and so to make a repetition of a like success by the like discreditable arts difficult if not impossible.

THE END.

Richard Clay & Sons, London and Bungay.

www.ingramcontent.com/pod-product-compliance
Lightning Source LLC
Chambersburg PA
CBHW021359230426
43666CB00006B/579